# No Other
# Gospel

# No Other
# Gospel

FINDING TRUE FREEDOM
*in the* MESSAGE *of* GALATIANS

# Carol J. Ruvolo

P U B L I S H I N G
P.O. BOX 817 • PHILLIPSBURG • NEW JERSEY 08865-0817

*Page design and typesetting by Lakeside Design Plus*

Printed in the United States of America

**Library of Congress Cataloging-in-Publication Data**

Ruvolo, Carol J., 1946–
    No other gospel : finding true freedom in the message of Galatians / Carol J. Ruvolo.
        p.    cm.
    Includes bibliographical references and index.
    ISBN-10: 0-87552-635-7 (pbk.)
    ISBN-13: 978-0-87522-635-5 (pbk.)
    1. Bible. N.T. Galatians—Textbooks.  I. Title.

BS2685.55.R88 2006
227'.40071—dc22
                                                        2006043286

*For Jean Kolysko,*
*dear friend and persistent encourager*

*My deepest gratitude goes out to*
*two very special couples,*

*Brendon and Joan O'Dowd*
*and*
*Andy and Amy Leong,*

*who read every word of the manuscript,*
*made wise suggestions and insightful comments,*
*and encouraged me to keep going.*
*What a blessing they have been and still are!*

# Contents

Long my imprisoned spirit lay,
Fast bound in sin and nature's night;
Thine eye diffused a quick'ning ray,
I woke, the dungeon flamed with light;
My chains fell off, my heart was free,
I rose, went forth, and followed Thee.

—Charles Wesley,
"And Can It Be That I Should Gain"

# Wait!
# Don't Skip This

Are you one of those folks who typically skips right past prefaces, forewords, and introductions to get to the "good stuff"? I am. And that's why I want to encourage you not to skip over this preface. It contains what is meant to be "good stuff" too—stuff that will enhance the benefit you'll derive from these lessons. So please take a minute or two to read and think about the information and suggestions here before diving in.

————— ❧ —————

This study of Galatians has grown out of a commitment to the Bible as the infallible, inerrant, authoritative, and entirely sufficient Word of God, and a conviction that Reformed theology is the clearest and most accurate restatement of biblical truth. The study format of this book will guide you through each portion of Paul's letter to the Galatians, enabling you to understand and apply the meaning of each passage.

Bible study is a serious task that involves a significant investment of time and energy. Preparing yourself to study effectively will help you reap the greatest benefit from that investment. Study when you are well rested and alert. Try to find a time and place that is quiet, free of distractions, and conducive to concentration. Use a loose-leaf or spiral notebook to take notes on what you read and to do the exercises in this study.

Approach Bible study as you would any task that requires thought and effort to do well. Don't be surprised if it challenges you and stretches your thinking. Expect it to be difficult at times but extremely rewarding.

Always begin your study with prayer. Ask the Lord to reveal sin in your life that needs to be confessed and cleansed, to help you concentrate on His truths, and to illumine your mind with understanding of what He has written. End your study with a prayer for opportunities to apply what you have learned and wisdom to recognize those opportunities when they occur.

Each lesson in this book is followed by three types of exercises: *Review*, *Application*, and *Digging Deeper*. The Review exercises will help you determine how well you understood the lesson material by giving you an opportunity to express the key points in your own words. The Application exercises encourage you to put your understanding of the material to work in your daily life. And the Digging Deeper exercises challenge you to pursue further study in certain key areas.

You should be able to find the answers to the Review questions in the lesson material, but please resist the temptation to copy words or phrases out of the lesson when you answer these questions. Work at putting these ideas into your own words. When you can do this, you know you have understood what you have read. It might help to ask yourself, "How would I explain this idea to someone else if I didn't have the book with me?"

If you don't have time to do all of the Application exercises, pray over them and ask the Lord to show you which one(s) He wants you to work on. Because you will be applying the lessons to your daily life, these applications should take some time and thought. Answering one of them well will benefit you more than answering all of them superficially.

Answers to the Application exercises should be very specific. Work at avoiding vague generalities. It might help to keep in mind that a specific application will provide specific answers to the questions who? what? when? where? and how? A vague generality will not. You can make applications in the areas of your thinking, your attitudes, and your behavior.

Digging Deeper exercises usually require a significant amount of time and effort to complete. They were designed to provide a challenge for mature Christians who are eager for more advanced study. However, new Christians should not automatically pass them by. The Holy Spirit may choose to use one of them to help you grow. Remember that all Christians grow by stretching beyond where they are right now. So if one or two of these exercises intrigue you, spend some time working on them. And do not hesitate to ask for help from your pastor, elders, teacher, or mature Christian friends.

As you work through this study, resist the temptation to compare yourself with other Christians in your group. The purpose of this study is to help you grow in your faith by learning and applying God's truth in your daily life—not to fill up a study book with brilliantly worded answers. If you learn and apply one element of God's truth in each lesson, you are consistently moving beyond where you were when you began.

Always remember that effective Bible study equips you to glorify God and enjoy Him forever. You glorify God when you live in such a way that those around you can look at you and see an accurate reflection of God's character and nature. You enjoy God when you are fully satisfied in His providential ordering of the circumstances in your life. When your life glorifies God and your joy is rooted in His providence, your impact on our fallen world will be tremendous.

# The Threat

JERUSALEM, A.D. 49:[1] The apostle Paul was mad. So mad, in fact, that he instinctively turned away from the messenger standing before him. It would not be right to blast the messenger because of his message, and Paul's rising rage warned him to withhold comment until he had cooled off.

"Go inside and find Barnabas. He'll see to it you're fed and housed while I work on a response." Paul waved the man toward a row of low buildings as he briskly set off for his own rented quarters.

The messenger had been traveling for weeks—all the way from Galatia by way of Antioch—and would no doubt welcome a good meal and a bed. Paul knew that the "Son of Encouragement" would take excellent care of the man's needs, leaving Paul free to deal with the needs of his message. With fingers itching for ink and parchment, he was already composing an irate response to the infuriating news the man had delivered.

Paul quickened his steps and focused his thoughts on the unexpected development that had suddenly intensified the threat to the gospel that had brought him to Jerusalem. The Judaizers, whose infiltration of the Antioch church with distorted teaching had precipitated the Council, were also targeting the infant congregations of Southern Galatia with the same hateful doctrine.

Paul fumed as he recalled the diligence with which he and Barnabas had taught the truths of the gospel to Jews and Gentiles alike throughout Galatia. He fumed as he recalled the physical pain and emotional anguish they had gladly endured for the sake of the elect in the cities they had visited. He fumed as he realized how quickly their work could be undermined by well-crafted lies. Had it all been in vain? Would the Judaizers succeed in destroying what they had built? No! At least, not if he had anything to say about it.

And he did indeed have something to say about it.

UNITED STATES OF AMERICA, A.D. 2006: Wendell McKinley was mad. So mad, in fact, that he instinctively turned away from the house when he stepped out of his car. It wouldn't be right to fire off the blistering e-mail letter he was already composing—the one he wanted to write hot and send smoking—before giving himself some time to cool off.

Wendell had just had lunch with an old friend—a charter member of one of the many churches he had been instrumental in planting. Almost two years ago, Wendell had joyfully handed over leadership responsibility to a gifted group of qualified men who shared a desire to see the church grow and have an impact on the surrounding community. But growth had been slow, community impact seemed minimal, and the men grew discouraged.

But then, out of the blue, thirty-four "refugees" from a nearby church-split visited one Sunday, kept coming back, and finally signed up en masse for the membership class. All thirty-four soon joined the church and quickly got involved in various ministries. The men Wendell had trusted to lead the church he had planted rejoiced in their conviction that God was, at long last, blessing their efforts.

Wendell's lunch partner wasn't rejoicing with them, however. He told Wendell that the thirty-four newcomers had coalesced into a persuasive clique and were systematically "converting" the church to a brand of works-righteousness that clearly perverted God's gospel of grace. They had influenced key leaders and laypeople to the extent that the teaching, discipling, and counseling ministries of the church had changed drastically over the past several months. To Wendell's request for specific examples, his old friend handed him a list of verbatim quotations he had copied from audio tapes of sermons and Sunday school classes.

Wendell didn't have to read very far before losing his appetite. Fighting a tide of rising fury, he assured his old friend that he would contact the church leaders at once and headed for home. Struggling to drive sanely and within the speed limit, Wendell fumed while remembering all the hard work and study, all the prayers and love, all the training, late nights, and hand-holding that had gone into that church. He fumed over the prospects of such a carefully laid solid foundation cracking and crumbling under the weight of persuasive deception. He fumed at the very idea that false teachers might succeed in destroying what God had used him to build. Had it all been in vain? Would another good church be brought down by bad doctrine? No! Wendell's right hand slammed hard against the steering wheel. Not if he had anything to say about it.

And Wendell did indeed have something to say about it.

What were the apostle Paul and Wendell McKinley so mad about? In a word, legalism.

Both men were committed to preaching God's gospel of grace. And the folks Paul and Wendell were mad at were distorting that gospel. They were not denying that faith in Christ was the way of salvation. They were simply affirming that there is more to it than that.

The Judaizers of Paul's day taught that the way to the truth and the life went through Judaism. They said that faith in Christ was indeed necessary for salvation and righteous living, but so were circumcision and law-keeping. The thirty-four newcomers to Wendell's old congregation argued that salvation required faith in Christ *and*—being baptized, joining the church, affirming the church's doctrinal statement, *and*—pledging to attend worship services at least three times a week, read their Bibles daily, memorize Scripture, pray an hour each day, share their faith regularly, *and*—giving up smoking, drinking, swearing, movies, TV, the Internet, ballgames on Sunday, mixed swimming, dating, luxurious living, *and*—the list goes on.

In effect, both groups were proclaiming that faith plus human works is the way to be saved and maintain good standing with God. That kind of teaching should make us as mad as it did Paul and Wendell.[2] Why? Because teaching like that does not proclaim God's gospel of grace. "Grace plus" is not grace. Teaching that proclaims Christ *plus anything* is another gospel.

The gospel of grace not only announces that we are saved wholly by grace and not by our own works. It also affirms that *apart from Christ* we can do nothing (John 15:1–5), that *in Him* we can do all things (Philippians 4:13), and that God made men and women dependent on Him *so that* "the surpassing greatness of the power will be of God and not from ourselves" (2 Corinthians 4:7). The gospel of grace gives all the glory to God. Legalism expects God to share His glory with fallen mankind. God says He will not give His glory to another or His praise to graven images (Isaiah 42:8).

The real issue in legalism is not *what* we do or don't do. It is more a matter of *how and why* we do what we do or don't do. Legalism is not just an obsession with merit and conduct. It is a denial of the all-equipping power of grace and a rejection of the God-honoring purpose of grace. Scot McKnight says that legalism is actually more about subtraction than it is about addition. It "adds" to the gospel, he says, "by subtracting the sufficiency of Christ and the Spirit."[3]

The brand of legalism practiced by the Judaizers of Paul's day was the most serious threat faced by the first-century church. That is because it targeted three facets of Christianity's essence: (1) apostolic authority (God speaking through specific chosen men), (2) justification (salvation by grace alone through faith alone in Christ alone), and (3) sanctification (pursuing holiness in the power of the Spirit for the glory of God). Paul responded urgently and decisively to this serious threat in his epistle to the Galatians. He defended his authority to speak for God in chapters 1–2, affirmed the nature of salvation in chapters 3–4, and clarified the role of obedience in chapters 5–6.

The letter resonates with an urgency that approaches severity. The apostle is righteously angry with his Galatian brethren who have "so quickly" been duped by subversive teaching. He includes no warm words of praise or thanksgiving for them. He does not gently advise them of their error and kindly direct them back to right doctrine. He acts more like an enraged father jerking his child out of the path of an oncoming truck after the child has been well instructed not to play in the street. The father's love propels his rescue effort even as the child's foolishness ignites his wrath.

Paul wrote in anger because he loved the Galatians. He was not about to stand quietly by and watch them reap the harvest of their foolish credulity. Paul had invested his life in them, wanted to see them bear fruit, and was not about to give up on them easily. The Galatians knew better than to play in the street. Paul had taught them that God's *saving grace* had broken sin's shackles and freed them from living in the shadow of death. He had taught them that God's *equipping grace* was sufficient and powerful to overcome the weakness of their flesh and equip them to fulfill their chief end of joyfully giving God glory. And he had taught them that *appropriating* God's grace required them to depend on Christ's work of redemption and to humbly submit to God's Holy Spirit.

And yet, they had foolishly stepped into the path of an oncoming truck labeled "Legalism." Why would they do such a thing? For the same reasons we do. No matter how well we know the truths of the gospel, most of us are attracted by legalism in some form. That is because legalism appeals to our hungry egos. We like to think we deserve our salvation and that our behavior as Christians earns favor with God. We have a hard time believing that the difference between us and the pagan next door is solely God's grace. After all, if we are saved and he is not, it *must* be because we *did* something he did not do. We also balk at the idea that our acceptance with God rests entirely on our union with Christ. Surely Christians who *do* more righteous things rank higher with God than those who slide by. We like being able to measure our holiness in terms of achievement and to think that God likes the "most holy" best.

As long as we remain fallen sinners plagued by hungry egos, we remain vulnerable to legalism's allure. But succumbing to its attraction will not fulfill our chief end as we walk through this world. Walking worthy of our high calling so that God gets the glory requires us to resist the enticement of legalism. Studying Paul's letter to the Galatians will help us do that.

## Notes

1. The "Jerusalem, A.D. 49" portion of this introduction presents a possible scenario for the conditions surrounding the writing of Paul's letter to the Galatians. Most of the specific events in this portion of the introduction are

*not* recorded in the Bible. Rather, they reflect two inferences drawn from what *is* recorded in the Bible. Those inferences are: (1) the book of Galatians was addressed to the churches established in Southern Galatia on Paul's first missionary journey; and (2) the book of Galatians was written from Jerusalem during the Jerusalem Council. Some of you may agree with that scenario, and some of you may not. That is to be expected since excellent Bible scholars disagree on when, where, and to whom Galatians was written. I have studied Galatians and Acts carefully, read the commentaries written by many of those excellent Bible scholars, and come to two conclusions: (1) Galatians was *most likely* written to the churches in Southern Galatia established during Paul's first missionary journey; and (2) Galatians was *probably* written while Paul was participating in the Jerusalem Council (A.D. 49–50) but before the issues regarding Gentile converts were finally resolved. I am not sure I am right, but this scenario looks most right to me now. Obviously, we do not need a definitive answer to when, where, and to whom Galatians was written in order to understand what Paul is saying and how it applies to us. If we did, God would have made sure that Paul told us.

2. The anger we are talking about here is righteous anger, of course. Righteous anger is anger about things that anger God. Righteous anger is not sinful in itself, but it can lead to sin when we respond to it wrongly. Paul admonishes Christians to "be angry, and yet do not sin; do not let the sun go down on your anger, and do not give the devil an opportunity" (Ephesians 4:26–27). Anger is a powerful emotion that leaves us highly vulnerable to sinful responses. Even when our anger is righteous, we need to

exercise self-discipline, in the power of the Holy Spirit, to control our thoughts, words, and actions so that we will respond righteously.

3. Scot McKnight, *Galatians*, The NIV Application Commentary (Grand Rapids, Mich.: Zondervan, 1995), 26.

*Primary Passage*
GALATIANS 1:1–9

*Supplementary Passages*
JEREMIAH 31:31–34
EZEKIEL 11:19–21; 36:22–28
JOHN 1:1–18
ACTS 9:1–31; 13:1–15:2
ROMANS 1:1–7
1 CORINTHIANS 3:10–11; 15:1–10
EPHESIANS 1:3–14; 2:19–22
PHILIPPIANS 1:12–20; 2:5–16; 3:1–11
COLOSSIANS 1:13–14
1 TIMOTHY 1:12–16
TITUS 2:11–14
HEBREWS 10:1–10
1 JOHN 4:9–10

Before reading the lesson material, please read the primary Scripture passage listed above and as many of the supplementary passages as time allows. Then briefly summarize in your notebook what you have read. (Do not go into detail. Limit your summary to a brief description of the people, events, and/or ideas discussed in the passages.)

# Battle Cry of a Freedom Fighter

*Paul's doctrine of justification by faith, as set forth in Gala-*
*tians and more completely in Romans, was forged in the con-*
*text of a life-and-death struggle with those who would pervert*
*the gospel by minimizing the decisive character of God's grace*
*in the person and work of his Son. —*TIMOTHY GEORGE

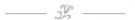

Have you noticed that many former "whatevers" tend to become the "whatevers'" most active opponents? If you know any former smokers, you know what I mean. Most of them work overtime trying to get others to quit. So do former drug abusers, workaholics, and overeaters.

Most of these people act out of compassion for those who are in bondage to something from which they themselves have been freed. They understand what it is like to live chained to an addiction, and they know, for a fact, that those chains can be broken. They want to help those who still groan under the weight of shackled potential, those whose spirits are still bound by futility, those whose "reason for being" is still being defined by oppressive constraint. They want folks to live free of whatever is tying them down.

Former "whatevers" are chain breakers and freedom fighters. They have broken free of some kind of bondage and now battle to help others do the same thing. When we read Galatians, we see that Paul was one of them. His "whatever" was legalism—a bondage more devastating than all others combined. Although all forms of bondage cripple Christian witness, legalism eats away at the heart of the gospel. It erases grace as the means of salvation and service, substitutes works as the way to find favor with God, and expects God to share His glory with fallen humanity.

Paul had been liberated from the chains of works-righteousness and fought to free others held captive by it. His only weapon was God's gospel of grace. He knew, from experience, that he needed no other. If God's grace had freed him, it could free anyone. Paul had once been an outstanding legalist because he had "a mind to put confidence in the flesh." He had been "circumcised the eighth day, of the nation of Israel, of the tribe of Benjamin, a Hebrew of Hebrews; as to the Law, a Pharisee; as to zeal, a persecutor of the church; as to the righteousness which is in the Law, found blameless" (Philippians 3:4–6).

But when Paul met Jesus Christ on the road to Damascus, his "confidence in the flesh" left him face down in the dirt.

God weakened his flesh, ransomed his heart, and shattered his bondage to legalism. In the ensuing days, God helped Paul see that he could be saved not by "a righteousness of [his] own derived from the Law," but only by having "the righteousness which comes from God on the basis of faith" in the atonement of Christ (v. 9).

Paul got the message, and he never forgot it. The heart of his preaching from that moment on was that no one could be justified (made right) with God by keeping the law (Romans 3:20). Instead, sinners must *receive* righteousness "as a gift by His grace through the redemption which is in Christ Jesus" (v. 24).

God also taught Paul that he could not walk worthy of his high calling by works-righteousness either. He had been called to be God's chosen instrument, an apostle, "to bear [His] name before the Gentiles and kings and the sons of Israel." And he had been told he would suffer greatly for the sake of that name (Acts 9:15–16). His worldly credentials had not qualified him for the job he had been given. His natural abilities would not equip and sustain him in the trials that were coming. His only qualification and power would be God's grace working in him.

God's Holy Spirit helped Paul understand his complete dependence on grace. That understanding transformed the apostle's self-image so thoroughly that he wrote to the Corinthians: "For I am the least of the apostles, and not fit to be called an apostle, because I persecuted the church of God. But by the grace of God I am what I am, and His grace toward me did not prove vain; but I labored even more than all of them, yet not I, but the grace of God with me" (1 Corinthians 15:9–10).[1]

Paul went on to preach God's gospel of grace faithfully in the region of Galatia. Many folks living in the cities of Pisidian Antioch, Iconium, Lystra, and Derbe received the Good

News with joy and were saved to serve God. They had run well for a time, but had inexplicably veered into the path of an oncoming truck labeled "Legalism." Judaizers had infiltrated their churches, undermined Paul's authority, and enticed them with law-keeping. Word got back to Paul, and he sprang into action. Seizing pen, ink, and parchment, he scrawled the terse, pointed sentences that open the book of Galatians.[2]

Stop now and reread Paul's words in Galatians 1:1–9 before going on with this lesson. I hope that as you read, you will hear, as I do, the battle cry of a freedom fighter.

## Remember Me?—The Apostle Paul

### *Galatians 1:1–2*

Paul's opening salvo reads like an e-mail message written "all-caps." It shouts loud enough to demand undivided attention. I am sure Paul did that intentionally because he saw himself as a lifeline for endangered brethren. Since their rescue depended upon hearing and heeding what he had to say, he began by asserting his apostolic authority.

Most of us, almost unconsciously, recognize legitimate authority and submit ourselves to it. When we approach an intersection and see that the traffic signal is out of order and that a police officer is giving direction to drivers, we comply. When I was a child and heard my father's voice calling me home, I went. When your work supervisor instructs you to complete Task A before beginning Task B, you plan your day accordingly.

But what do we do when authoritative directions conflict? What if the traffic signal is working and "red," but a police officer is motioning for you to keep moving? What about when my father called me home an hour before the time my mother said I could stay out? What if *your* supervisor says, "Do Task A first," but then *her* supervisor says to you, "Do Task B first"?

That is precisely the predicament the Galatians were in. The apostle Paul had preached the gospel to them, and they had accepted it. Then other authoritative teachers had come and "corrected" Paul's gospel, and they had accepted that too. Then they had received an angry letter from Paul saying that they had been deceived by the other teachers into believing "another gospel," which was no gospel at all. Both Paul and the other teachers seemed to be godly, intelligent men who argued their cases plausibly and winsomely. Whom should they believe? Whom should they follow?

Paul commanded them to listen to him because he spoke with the authority of a Christ-appointed apostle,[3] whereas the other teachers did not. Christ-appointed apostles were men who had been particularly chosen, equipped, and sent to proclaim divine truth "not . . . from men nor through the agency of man, but through Jesus Christ and God the Father, who raised Him from the dead" (1:1). Christ-appointed apostles were the final authority on subjects about which God had revealed His will. On those subjects, they did not speak their own thoughts or the thoughts of any other human beings. Rather, they were "moved by the Holy Spirit [to speak] from God" (2 Peter 1:20–21). When people disagree with a Christ-appointed apostle concerning revelation from God, they are wrong.

Paul did not assert his apostolic authority to thwart personal attacks. He acknowledged to the Philippians that some were preaching the gospel "from envy and strife, . . . out of selfish ambition rather than from pure motives, thinking to cause me distress in my imprisonment." But he did not tell the Philippians to shun or ignore them. Instead, he rejoiced that "in every way, whether in pretense or in truth, Christ is proclaimed" (Philippians 1:15–18). Paul was not all that concerned about the way others treated him. But he was passionately concerned about how they treated the gospel.

He wielded the weapon of his apostolic authority against opposing teachers in Galatia, not because they were opposing him personally, but because they were undermining the gospel he preached. He did not hesitate to defend and assert "the independence of his apostleship in order to defend the gospel."[4]

## The Gospel Truth

### *(Galatians 1:3–5)*

The Galatians were clearly confused about gospel truth. Although they had responded in faith to Paul's proclamation, they did not understand it well enough to recognize and reject another gospel, which was no gospel at all. Paul gave them a masterful refresher course: "Grace to you and peace from God our Father and the Lord Jesus Christ, who gave Himself for our sins so that He might rescue us from this present evil age, according to the will of our God and Father, to whom be the glory forevermore. Amen" (1:3–5).

Do you see what Paul has done there? What looks like a simple greeting is, in reality, a one-sentence statement of the heart of the gospel. It tells us that the gospel *consists* in grace and peace from God our Father and the Lord Jesus Christ; that it was *accomplished* when Jesus gave Himself for our sins according to the will of our God and Father; that it *resulted* in rescuing us from this present evil age; and that its *purpose* is to glorify God forever. It is indeed a "masterful refresher course"—not because it re-preaches exhaustively what Paul had taught the

Galatians—but because it supplies four critical touchstones to help them remember what he had taught them.

Touchstone #1 is the phrase "grace and peace." Intent as Paul was on freeing his brethren from the grip of legalism, it is no surprise that the word "grace" stands first in this sentence. Grace contradicts and opposes all aspects of legalism. Grace provides peace with God to unworthy, helpless, hate-filled sinners who cannot merit it and will not seek it (Romans 5:6, 8, 10). Grace comes from God the Father and the Lord Jesus Christ as a gift, freely bestowed rather than earned (6:23). Grace gives cursed men and women what God requires of them to make peace with Him when they lack the desire and ability to do so themselves (5:1). The gospel truth Paul had preached to the Galatians consisted of gracious means to the end of peace with God and stood in stark contrast to the "other gospel" of legalism.

Touchstone #2 is the reminder of how God accomplished the salvation of sinners. Jesus gave Himself for our sins according to the will of our God and Father. Jesus acted in submission to the plan of the Father to redeem a people for His own possession by satisfying God's righteous requirements on our behalf (Philippians 2:5–8; Titus 2:14). He lived in perfect obedience to all of God's law and gave us the credit for all of His righteousness (Philippians 3:9; Hebrews 5:8–10). He took our sin upon Himself on the cross, absorbed all of God's holy wrath against our sin, and shifted our curse to Himself (Romans 5:9; 2 Corinthians 5:21; Galatians 3:13). God announced His complete satisfaction with Jesus' substitutionary work on our behalf by raising Him from the dead and exalting Him to the right hand of God where He exercises all power and authority as Lord of all (Acts 2:29–36; Romans 4:25). Once again, gospel truth clearly opposes the teaching of legalism. Salvation is accomplished wholly by divine action. Our works contribute nothing to it.

Touchstone #3 is the word "rescue." Gospel truth announces the good news that salvation results in sinners' being rescued from this present evil age.[5] We are saved to live "in this age the life of the age to come."[6] How does salvation do that? It replaces hard hearts of stone that are unresponsive to God with soft hearts of flesh that desire to do His will (Ezekiel 11:19–20; 36:26–27). It shifts our focus from the things of this earth to the things above (Colossians 3:1–2). It turns us away from ungodliness and worldly desires and purifies us as a people for Christ's own possession, zealous for good deeds (Titus 2:11–14). Our rescue from this present evil age to serve God in holiness is empowered by God's Holy Spirit living within us (1 Corinthians 15:10; Philippians 2:12–13; 4:13). It cannot be achieved through the false doctrines of legalism.

Touchstone #4 crystallizes the real issue at stake in Paul's battle with legalism: Who gets the glory? The gospel truth, which affirms that salvation and Christian living are thoroughly gracious, glorifies God (1 Corinthians 10:31; Ephesians 1:3–14; 1 Peter 4:10–11). The false doctrines of legalism, which affirm that human effort contributes to right standing with God, glorify man.

Paul's masterful refresher course containing four critical touchstones serves as a rebuke as well as a reminder. My guess is that Paul wrote that sentence quickly and easily without laboring unduly over its content and construction. He could do that because he understood the gospel so well. If the Galatians had understood the gospel *so well*, they might not have succumbed so easily to another gospel, which was no gospel at all. Knowing the truth is the best way to recognize error.

False teachers prey on immature, uninstructed, indifferent Christians. Gullible, credulous Christians welcomed bad doctrine into the cities of Galatia because they lacked the deep knowledge of gospel truth that would equip them to recognize and refute error. And they were not alone. Bad doctrine runs rampant today because superficiality is alive and well in our churches.

How well do you understand gospel truth? Well enough to distill it down to one masterful sentence containing enough critical touchstones to guard you from error? If not, give prayerful heed to Application exercise 3 at the end of this lesson.

## How Dare You Desert the Gospel of Grace!

### *Galatians 1:6–9*

Churches are rarely destroyed by outside attack. In fact, history has demonstrated that outside attack tends to *strengthen* Christ's church in the world. The most cunning and successful opponents of Christianity do not stand outside our assemblies and hurl insults at us. They do not oppose us in the media, pass laws against free expression of our beliefs, or burn down our buildings. Instead, they worm their way into our fellowship, gain our trust, and proceed to pervert God's gospel of grace. They are dangerous because they appear to be leading people to Christ while actually impeding the way of salvation by grace.

Paul was astounded that the Galatians had been so easily duped by such deceivers. His missionary trip through the cities of Galatia has been accurately described by many commentators as "wildly successful." Acts 13:1–14:23 indicates that the Galatians' response to his preaching had been sincere and genuine, that they had been taught well, and that they had been left with good leadership. Paul must have been overflowing with joy when he reported to the disciples at Antioch all the things "God had done with them and how He had opened a door of faith to the Gentiles" (14:27). And that, no doubt, explains his indignant response to the news that the Galatians were defecting to legalism.

"I am amazed," he wrote to them, "that you are so quickly deserting Him who called you by the grace of Christ, for a different gospel; which is really not another; only there are some who are disturbing you and want to distort the gospel of Christ" (Galatians 1:6–7).

The Greek word translated "deserting" is a present-tense verb that was first used in a military context to describe traitors. Later it was applied to those who converted from one religion or philosophy to another. Paul's word usage here tells us that although he was furious at their defection, he had not given up hope. He saw them as "in the process" of accepting a different gospel and thus still open to rebuke and correction.

When Paul said the Galatians were deserting God's gospel of grace "for a different gospel; which is really not another," he used the Greek words *heteros* ("different") and *allos* ("another"). Although both words could be translated with the English words "different" or "another," they are not synonyms in Greek. *Heteros* means "another of a different class or kind," whereas *allos* means "another of the same class or kind."

The distinction between them is illustrated well in an event from my childhood. During a family meal at my grandparents' home, I suddenly realized that the adults at the table were eating steak while the children had been served hamburger patties. Although my hamburger patty was quite tasty, I wanted some steak. So I ate slowly, waited until all the hamburger was gone, and then asked my father for another piece of meat. He responded by telling me he was sorry, but there was none left. He assumed I was asking him for *allos* meat—another of the same kind. But I was, in fact, asking him for *heteros* meat—another of a different kind.

By using these two words in his rebuke of the Galatians, Paul asserted unequivocally that there is only one gospel. Forsaking the gospel of grace for a *heteros* gospel is disastrous because there is no such thing as an *allos* gospel. Replacing the gospel of grace with a gospel of works denies God's revealed truth.

Anyone who comes preaching a gospel different from the one God authorized Paul to preach is perverting God's revealed truth and must not be tolerated. "Even if we, or an angel from heaven, should preach to you a gospel contrary to what we have preached to you, he is to be accursed!" (1:8), Paul exclaimed. "As we have said before, so I say again now, if any man is preaching to you a gospel contrary to what you received, he is to be accursed!" The word translated "accursed," *anathema*, means "set apart and devote to destruction." This is the gravest of responses to the gravest of sins.

We can infer from Paul's statement that the gospel is a fixed body of truth that cannot be changed, and that its authority rests in its source, not its messenger. He goes so far as to submit himself, his fellow apostles, and even the angels in heaven to the gospel's authority. John MacArthur describes him as vehemently reaching "for the most fanciful possibilities imaginable to make his point that absolutely no messenger, no matter how seemingly godly and good, should be believed or followed if his teaching does not square with God-revealed apostolic doctrine. The truth outranks anyone's credentials, and every teacher or preacher must be evaluated on the basis of what he says, not who he is."[7]

The New Testament speaks of only two general categories of people whom God devotes to destruction: those who do not love the Lord (1 Corinthians 16:22), and false teachers (Galatians 1:8–9; 1 Timothy 1:18–20). Those who do not love the Lord and those who pervert gospel truth desecrate the glory of God and impugn His sovereign majesty. But they will not get away with it. They will reap what they sow—utter destruction in separation from God.

## Notes

1. It is interesting to note that by the time Paul wrote 1 Timothy, his confidence in himself had further disintegrated. In 1 Timothy 1:15, he refers to himself not as the least of the apostles, but as the chief of sinners. Apparently Paul did *not* "feel better about himself" the longer he was a Christian. Instead, he seems to have grown more keenly aware of his own inability to serve God "in the flesh," and he appears to have developed an increasing sense of his complete dependence on grace the longer he served Him.

2. I am aware that Paul usually dictated his letters to a scribe (*amanuensis*). However, Galatians 6:11 leads me to think he *might* have written this entire letter (not just the conclusion) in his own hand. That would certainly fit with the tone and urgency of the letter.

3. "Apostle" was the term used by Jesus to designate men who had been personally chosen, called, commissioned, and authorized to teach in His name. The term was not used to refer to believers in general, as was the term "disciple," but was a specialized term applied to a unique group who had

no successors (John R. W. Stott, *The Message of Galatians*, The Bible Speaks Today [Downers Grove, Ill.: InterVarsity, 1968], 13). Although the word "apostle" can be used in a general sense to refer to "sent ones," Paul uses it here in Galatians to refer to those men appointed by Christ to speak revealed truth from God.

4. Philip Graham Ryken, *Galatians*, Reformed Expository Commentary (Phillipsburg, N.J.: P&R Publishing, 2005), 6.

5. My thanks to Brendon O'Dowd for pointing out that the Greek word translated "rescue" here is not a mild one. It carries the idea of "ripping out," or "a violent takeover." Rescuing sinners from this present evil age was no pleasant stroll in the park for God. It was truly a bloody deliverance from a vicious enemy.

6. Stott, *The Message of Galatians*, 18.

7. John MacArthur Jr., *Galatians*, The MacArthur New Testament Commentary (Chicago: Moody Press, 1987), 16.

## E x e r c i s e s

### REVIEW

1. Read Acts 9:1–31; 22:1–21; 26:9–23; and Philippians 3:1–14. Describe the changes in Paul that resulted from his salvation. How does Paul account for these changes?

2. What distinguishes Christ-appointed apostles from other people? What were Paul's reasons for emphasizing his standing as a Christ-appointed apostle to the Galatians? Do you think it was necessary for him to do this? Explain your answer.

3. List and briefly explain each of the four critical touchstones contained in Galatians 1:3–5 that help us recall the essential elements of the gospel.

4. How is Paul's "masterful refresher course" in Galatians 1:3–5 a rebuke as well as a reminder?

5. Should we fear false teaching more than persecution? Explain your answer.

6. Read Acts 13:1–14:23. How does this passage help you understand Paul's attitude toward the Galatians in 1:6–9?

7. Distinguish between the Greek words *heteros* and *allos*. Then explain the significance of Paul's usage of those two words in Galatians 1:6–7.

8. Discuss the significance of Paul's curse in Galatians 1:8–9.

## APPLICATION

1. This week begin memorizing one or more of the following Scripture passages:

   1 Corinthians 15:10 (If you are up to the challenge, memorize vv. 1–10.)

   2 Corinthians 3:5–6

   Titus 2:11–14

2. This week in your prayer time, use 1 Corinthians 15:1–10 and Philippians 2:5–16 to help you thank God for the grace of salvation and for the grace that equips you to glorify and enjoy Him in all circumstances of life.

3. How well do you understand the gospel? Answer the following questions after considering the accompanying Scripture passages. When, where, and with whom did the gospel origi-

nate (Ephesians 3:11; 2 Timothy 1:9; Titus 1:1–2; Hebrews 13:20)? What prevents human beings from relating rightly to God (Isaiah 6:1–5; 59:2; Romans 3:9–20)? How does the gospel establish a right relationship between God and human beings (Romans 3:21–28; 5:9; 8:3–4; 2 Corinthians 5:21; Ephesians 1:3–14; Hebrews 5:9–10)? How is the gospel communicated (Romans 10:14–15; 2 Timothy 3:14–15)? How is the gospel received (John 6:37, 44, 65; Philippians 3:9; Ephesians 2:8–9)? What does the gospel accomplish (Romans 5:1–2; 2 Corinthians 3:18; Ephesians 2:10; Titus 2:11–14; 3:4–7; 1 Peter 1:3–5, 9)? What is the ultimate purpose of the gospel (Isaiah 43:7, 20–21; Matthew 5:16; Ephesians 1:6, 12, 14; 1 Peter 2:9)?

Using your answers to the above questions, distill the gospel into one sentence containing the gospel's essential elements. How might memorizing this sentence protect you from falling under the influence of false teachers?

## DIGGING DEEPER

1. Timothy George, in his commentary on Galatians, supposes that first-century Judaizers may have presented their spurious doctrine in letters or sermons similar to the following:

   "Dear brothers of Galatia, we greet you in the Name of our Lord Jesus Christ! We have heard how through the ministry of Brother Paul you have been converted from the worship of dumb idols to serve the true and living God of Israel. We are glad you have made such a good beginning, but we are afraid that there are some very important things about the Gospel Paul has omitted to tell you. We ourselves come from the church at Jerusalem which is directed by the apostles Jesus called and ordained. Paul though is an upstart. Why, he never even knew Jesus while he was on earth and was certainly never commissioned by him as an apostle. True, Paul did visit Jerusalem just after he stopped persecuting us, and there he learned the ABCs of the Christian faith from the true apostles. But the message he now preaches bears no resemblance to theirs. I don't imagine he even told you about circumcision! Why, this is the very way God made it possible for you Gentiles to become a part of the New Israel. Jesus did not come to abolish the law but to fulfill it. Circumcision is just as important as baptism—nay, more important, for it will introduce you to a higher plane of Christian living. If you will observe this holy ordinance of the law, God will be pleased with you. We are just now forming a new association of law-observant churches, and we would love for Galatia to be represented! We are the true Christians. Jesus, our great example, pleased the Father by fulfilling the law and so can you!" (Timothy George, *An Exegetical and Theological Exposition of Galatians*, The New American Commentary [Nashville: Broadman and Holman, 1994], 95–96).

Research what the Bible teaches about Paul's claim to be an apostle and about the gracious nature of salvation. Then write a response to the above supposed communication. Support your points with specific scriptural references. Do not hesitate to seek input from your pastor, elders, other church leaders, or wise Christian acquaintances.

2. Writing almost forty years ago, John R. W. Stott said, "We live in an age in which it is considered very narrow-minded and intolerant to have any clear and strong opinions of one's own, let alone to disagree sharply with anybody else" (Stott, *The Message of Galatians*, 26). Do you think his words are

more or less relevant to our own day than they were to the day in which they were written? Explain your answer using personal or cultural illustrations. Then explain the impact you think this characteristic of our age has had on Christians—particularly in regard to their understanding and proclamation of the gospel of grace.

*Primary Passage*
GALATIANS 1:10–2:10

*Supplementary Passages*
ISAIAH 49:1–6
JEREMIAH 1:4–10
ACTS 8:1–3; 9:1–31; 11:27–30; 15:1–35; 16:1–3; 22:6–
    21; 26:12–18
ROMANS 2:1–11
1 CORINTHIANS 7:17–20; 9:1, 19–23; 15:3–11
2 CORINTHIANS 4:1–6; 11:30–33
EPHESIANS 1:11
PHILIPPIANS 3:1–11
2 PETER 1:20–21

Before reading the lesson material, please read the primary
Scripture passage listed above and as many of the supplementary passages as time allows. Then briefly summarize in
your notebook what you have read. (Do not go into detail.
Limit your summary to a brief description of the people,
events, and/or ideas discussed in the passages.)

# Independence and Harmony

*Paul's . . . gospel . . . was neither an invention . . . nor a tradition . . . , but a revelation. . . . It was not "his" because he had made it up but because it had been uniquely revealed to him.* —JOHN R. W. STOTT

Several women of my church and a few of their guests recently returned from our first annual women's retreat. For twenty-four blessed hours, we soaked in the beauty of God's creation in the mountains near Santa Fe and soaked up the marvel of the truth of His grace. Our teacher, Paige Benton (by way of video tape), had taught insightfully from God's Word how His grace saves us, strengthens us, sends us, and secures us.[1] Her powerful words had a powerful impact, and we all left the mountains with a much firmer grip on this incomparable doctrine.

Interestingly, as most of us sat together in church the next day, we heard our pastor repeat several truths we had just heard from Paige—a couple of them almost verbatim! A few knowing smiles and raised eyebrows were exchanged between us, and then my best friend passed me a note which read, "Was he at the retreat?"

He wasn't, of course. Paige's talks and the Sunday sermon were produced independently. The videos had been recorded two years before our retreat, and my pastor had not seen them before he prepared his sermon. Yet without any collaborative effort, preacher and teacher had harmonized beautifully. How did that happen? Simple. Paige and my pastor get their material from the same place and submit themselves to the same Holy Spirit.

This type of thing happens all the time at my church. And it probably happens just as often at yours. We should *expect* it to happen if we are listening to godly preachers and teachers. Non-collaborative harmony reflects independent commitment to the truths of God's Word and independent willingness to be led by His Spirit. Godly preachers and teachers do not necessarily have to consult with each other to proclaim God's truth harmoniously. Harmony flows from consultation with God.

Paul emphasized this supernatural reality when he defended his apostolic authority against the false teachers of legalism. In defending his independence from the original Twelve, he affirmed that the gospel he preached was no different from theirs.

## An Independent Apostle

### *(Galatians 1:10–24)*

Do you remember why the false gospel of legalism was the most serious threat faced by the first-century church? If you said, "Because it targeted three aspects of Christianity's essence:

apostolic authority, justification, and sanctification," put a gold star on the title page of your book. Paul addresses each of these aspects of Christianity's essence in the book of Galatians. He affirms his authority to speak for God in chapters 1–2, preaches salvation by grace alone through faith alone in Christ alone in chapters 3–4, and exhorts us to pursue holiness in the power of the Holy Spirit for the glory of God in chapters 5–6.

His approach was undoubtedly dictated by the attacks of the Judaizers who claimed that Paul was not a Christ-appointed apostle, that he did not preach a true gospel, and that the gospel he preached led to licentious living. They insinuated that Paul was not speaking for God but "tickling the ears" of Gentiles when he said that they could be made right with God without keeping the law. They said he was telling folks what they wanted to hear. They said he was preaching a watered down gospel specifically crafted to make non-Jewish converts. They said he was a "man-pleaser" whose gospel of grace without works ignored God's command to "be holy as I am holy."

Paul responded vehemently to these attacks—not because he was miffed at their remarks about him, but because he was incensed by their distortion of truth. His outrage, controlled but quite evident, surges through his defense of his apostolic authority.

> For am I now seeking the favor of men, or of God? Or am I striving to please men? If I were still trying to please men, I would not be a bond-servant of Christ. For I would have you know, brethren, that the gospel which was preached by me is not according to man. For I neither received it from man, nor was I taught it, but I received it through a revelation of Jesus Christ. (1:10–12)

31

Paul wanted to know, first of all, whether the curse he had just leveled against the foes of the gospel supported their assessment of his motives for preaching. Do "man-pleasers" go around pronouncing anathemas[2] against other teachers? Hardly. Paul implies that he had been a man-pleaser at one time but was no longer. Now his sole ambition was to please his Lord Jesus Christ.

But wait a minute. Didn't Paul tell the Corinthians that he characteristically accommodated himself to all men? Didn't he say that he reached people by becoming like them? To the Jews, he became as a Jew. To those under the law, he became as under the law. To those without law, he became as without law. To the weak he became weak. Didn't he say, "I have become all things to all men, so that I may by all means save some" (1 Corinthians 9:19–22)? Were the Judaizers right? Was Paul talking out of both sides of his mouth? Of course not!

Paul's words to the Corinthians describe his willingness to accommodate *himself* to all men. He would endure any hardship, distress, or embarrassment to get people to listen. But there is a big difference between accommodating ourselves and accommodating the gospel. Paul was willing to be all things to all men to get a hearing. But he never changed gospel truth to get a response.

The Judaizers had accused him of playing fast and loose with the gospel, and that accusation had to be countered—not for Paul's sake, but for the sake of the gospel he preached. If the Judaizers succeeded in discrediting Paul, they would also succeed in discrediting his gospel. If the false gospel of legalism supplanted the gospel of grace, God's divine purpose of blessing all nations through Abraham's seed would be thwarted (Genesis 12:3). The "barrier of the dividing wall" between Jew and Gentile would remain firmly intact, preventing the two groups from being made "into one new man," reconciled "in one body to God" through the work of His Son (Ephesians 2:11–16).

Several times in the Scripture, the outworking of God's divine purpose seems to teeter on the brink of extinction, as it does here. And every time, our sovereign God raises up a strong saint to stand in the gap. That is because He knows the end from the beginning and will accomplish all His good pleasure (Isaiah 46:9–11). God chose Paul from eternity past not only to be saved by His grace and take the gospel of grace to the Gentiles, but also to stand in the gap and deflect attempts to pervert the gospel with legalism.

Proclaiming truth often entails refuting error. And refuting error requires establishing authority. If Paul were effectively to counter the first century's most serious threat to the gospel of grace, he first had to show that he was indeed a Christ-appointed apostle. He did this by describing the independence of his conversion to Christ and his calling to preach.[3]

> For you have heard of my former manner of life in Judaism, how I used to persecute the church of God beyond measure and tried to destroy it; and I was advancing in Judaism beyond many of my contemporaries among my countrymen, being more extremely zealous for my ancestral traditions. But when God, who had set me apart even from my mother's womb and called me through His grace, was pleased to reveal His Son in me so that I might preach Him among the Gentiles, I did not immediately consult with flesh and blood, nor did I go up to Jerusalem to those who were apostles before me; but I went away to Arabia, and returned once more to Damascus. (Galatians 1:13–17)

Paul's conversion to Christianity was absolutely astounding. All conversions are miraculous, of course, but Paul's conversion was exponentially miraculous. John Stott describes Saul of Tarsus before his conversion as "a bigot and a fanatic, whole-hearted in his devotion to Judaism and in his persecution of Christ and the church. Now a man in that mental and emotional state is in no mood to change his mind, or even to have it changed for him by men. No conditioned reflex or other psychological device could convert a man in that state. Only God could reach him—and God did!"[4] John Brown captures the essence of Stott's description when he affirms that "divine grace never had a more glorious trophy."[5]

Paul's conversion to Christ came simultaneously with his call to preach. He had been "set apart"—through God's gracious choice—to receive divine revelation about Jesus Christ and proclaim it to the Gentiles. That put him on a par with men such as Isaiah, Jeremiah, Peter, James, and John (Isaiah 49:1–6; Jeremiah 1:4–10; John 1:35–49). His commissioning for service by the risen Christ on the road to Damascus made him just as much a spokesman for God as any of the Old Testament prophets or the New Testament Twelve.

Paul goes on to assert that he did not learn the gospel from the other apostles (or from any other human agency), but received it by direct revelation from God. He went to Arabia, not to Jerusalem, immediately after his conversion and call, and remained there for three years.

When he did finally visit Jerusalem "to become acquainted with Cephas [a.k.a. Peter]," he stayed a mere fifteen days and "did not see any other of the apostles except James, the Lord's brother."[6] Paul assured the Galatians that at the time he departed for the regions of Syria and Cilicia he was "still unknown by sight" to the Christian congregations of Judea that "were glorifying God" because of what they had heard regarding his astonishing conversion.

What Paul did in these verses was to present a "selective autobiography" that effectively countered the Judaizers' assaults. He pinpointed significant events in his life that confirmed his apostolic authority. In the three years following his conversion—years in which his concept of the gospel was established—he spent almost no time in Jerusalem and even less time with the Twelve. No one in Arabia at that time could have taught him the gospel he understood and proclaimed so well. The facts of Paul's life validate his assertion that he had received the gospel by divine revelation of Christ just as the Twelve had. He was, therefore, justified in representing himself as their equal rather than as their disciple.

## No Different Gospel

### *(Galatians 2:1–10)*

Validating Paul's apostolic authority, however, required more than affirming his independent receipt of the gospel. It also compelled him to show that the gospel he preached to the Gentiles was the very same gospel the Twelve proclaimed to the Jews. He showed this by recounting another visit he had made to Jerusalem.[7]

> Then after an interval of fourteen years I went up again to Jerusalem with Barnabas, taking Titus along also. It was because of a revelation that I went up; and I submitted to them the gospel which I preach among the Gentiles, but I did so in private to those who were of reputation, for fear that I might be running, or had run, in vain. (2:1–2)

Paul's words to the Galatians do not reflect any insecure fear that he might have been preaching the wrong gospel since his conversion. Rather, they reflect his keen insight into the false teachers' methods. He knew that "divide and conquer" was one of their favorite ploys. If they could drive a wedge between Paul and the Twelve, the false doctrine of legalism stood a good chance of annihilating the true gospel of grace. But God was not about to let that happen.

Paul said that he went to Jerusalem "because of a revelation." Whether that revelation initiated or validated his decision to travel is not all that important. What matters most is that Paul followed God's lead. The time had come to stand firm in the gap, and Paul did not hesitate. I cannot help but wonder if his choice of traveling companions was also determined by the revelation. Barnabas, a Christian Jew, and Titus, a Christian Gentile, pictured the unity inherent in the gospel Paul preached. Titus had not become a Christian by first becoming a Jew. And Barnabas and Paul considered him a true brother. They all must have known he would serve as a test case when they got to Jerusalem. If Paul's gospel of grace were erroneous, the Twelve would surely have insisted that Titus be circumcised right there on the spot.

Although J. B. Lightfoot refers to Galatians 2:3–5 as a "shipwreck of grammar,"[8] most commentators understand it to teach that Titus was neither encouraged nor compelled to be circumcised. Paul indicated that the Judaizers made their case by having "false brethren secretly brought in, who had sneaked in to spy out our liberty which we have in Christ Jesus, in order to bring us into bondage" (2:4). Timothy George says that the words Paul used here characterize the Judaizers as carrying on conspiratorial activity for sinister purposes.[9] Although Paul's words do not tell us precisely what the Judaizers did, his language communicated clearly that their behavior was neither honest nor honorable.

Paul went on to say that they failed in their efforts. "But we did not yield in subjection to them for even an hour, so that the truth of the gospel would remain with you" (v. 5). The word translated "yield" is a military term Paul probably chose to underscore the importance and seriousness of his stand against the "false brethren." He understood the connection between God's truth and freedom. He knew that the truth of the gospel produces real freedom—not freedom from God's holy requirements, but freedom to live by the power of His Holy Spirit so that He gets the glory. Paul stood firm against the false brethren because he knew that legalistic attempts to pad the gospel with works produce the worst kind of bondage.

The problem with legalism is not that it calls people to obey God's law, but that it views obedience as a means of gaining favor with God. Legalism appeals to our flesh because it gives us a false sense of control, a false sense of worthiness, and a false sense of security. "Keeping the rules," is something *we* do, something we *feel good* about, and something we think merits *favor with God*. Legalism evacuates the gospel's promise and hope by denying the truth of substitutionary atonement.

The gospel proclaims that Jesus Christ is the means by which we have favor with God. His perfect life and atoning death make those who trust Him right with God. Those who exercise God-given faith to repent and believe in Jesus Christ are accepted in the Beloved, and receive the gift of His indwelling Spirit. His work on our behalf and in our lives frees us to obey, not to earn His favor, but to give Him glory.

This is the gospel Paul preached, and the leaders of the church in Jerusalem affirmed that it was no different from the gospel they preached. Paul said:

> . . . seeing that I had been entrusted with the gospel to the uncircumcised, just as Peter had been to the circumcised (for He who effectually worked for Peter in his apostleship to the circumcised effectually worked for me also to the Gentiles), and recognizing the grace that had been given to me, James and Cephas [a.k.a. Peter] and John, who were reputed to be pillars, gave to me and Barnabas the right hand of fellowship, so that we might go to the Gentiles and they to the circumcised. They only asked us to remember the poor—the very thing I also was eager to do. (2:7–10)

Paul's unqualified acceptance by the leadership in Jerusalem evidences the divine work of non-collaborative harmony. Although they had had little contact with each other, they spoke with one voice. They could extend the right hand of fellowship to each other, confident that the message proclaimed to both Jew and Gentile was one and the same. They could go separate ways to reach diverse people with the true gospel of grace. And as they went, they would be as unified in the practical outworking of truth as they were in their doctrine. As Jews and Gentiles were saved and joined together in one body in Christ, Paul would gladly instruct them to meet the needs of the poor without prejudice.

### *Notes*

1. At our first retreat, we watched video tapes of Paige Benton's teaching at the Presbyterian Church in America Western Regional WIC Conference held in Denver, Colorado, September 28–30, 2001. These tapes are entitled *Grace Saves*

*Us, Grace Strengthens Us, Grace Sends Us,* and *Grace Secures Us.* They are available from Master Media One, Ltd. (770–287–0322; masmedia@mindspring.com). Miss Benton, by the way, has since become Mrs. Brown.

2. You may recall from lesson 1 that *anathema* means "set apart or devote to destruction."

3. Since Paul was an apostle, his calling and commissioning to preach were distinctive. He received the Word of God directly because he was an instrument through whom divine revelation would be disclosed. Our study of God's truth and our training for service, while dependent on the same Spirit, come from a completed Bible, not new inspiration. Along with our private study of the Word, we are in large part dependent on Spirit-gifted teachers and preachers. We should not assume the same independence that the apostle Paul experienced in his training for ministry.

4. John R. W. Stott, *The Message of Galatians,* The Bible Speaks Today (Downers Grove, Ill.: InterVarsity, 1968), 31–32.

5. John Brown, *Galatians: A Geneva Series Commentary* (1853; reprint, Carlisle, Pa.: Banner of Truth, 2001), 68.

6. James, the Lord's brother, was not one of the original twelve Christ-appointed apostles. In fact, he was not a believer until after the death and resurrection of Jesus. Yet he has been considered by many to be an apostle for several reasons, including the following: Paul refers to him as an apostle here in Galatians; Jesus appeared to him after the resurrection and apparently personally commissioned him to preach; James was a leader in the church in Jerusalem; and he wrote a book of the Bible.

7. A great deal of the written commentary on Galatians 2:1–10 is devoted to discussing (debating?) whether the trip Paul refers to here corresponds to the "relief" visit recorded in Acts 11:27–30 or to the Jerusalem Council recorded in Acts 15:1–35. Many of these discussions are fascinating, and the issue itself is important for a variety of reasons—none of which is especially pertinent to the theme I have chosen to emphasize in this lesson. If you are interested, by all means, study the commentaries, take a position, and join the debate. But for the study at hand simply focus on Paul's *purpose* for this Jerusalem visit.

8. Quoted in Timothy George, *An Exegetical and Theological Exposition of Galatians*, The New American Commentary (Nashville: Broadman and Holman, 1994), 141.

9. Ibid., 148.

### E x e r c i s e s

REVIEW

1. Explain how "non-collaborative harmony" reflects God at work in His church.

2. Describe the threat posed by the false gospel of legalism to the first-century church.

3. Read 1 Corinthians 9:19–23. Does Paul's description of his ministry method in these verses contradict what he says in Galatians 1:10–24? Explain.

4. What was Paul's primary motive in countering the accusations leveled against him by the Judaizers?

5. How does Paul's "selective autobiography" in Galatians 1:10–2:10 establish his apostolic authority to speak for God?

6. Describe the connection between freedom and God's truth.

7. Think and discuss (optional): Do you agree with John Brown that "divine grace never had a more glorious trophy" than Paul? Why or why not? Support your reasoning with Scripture.

## APPLICATION

1. This week review previous memory verses and begin memorizing one or more of the following Scripture passages:

   Ephesians 1:11
   2 Peter 1:20–21
   1 Corinthians 9:19–23

2. This week in your prayer time, use Ephesians 2:11–22 to help you appreciate and thank God for the way He has worked in history, through direct revelation to prophets and apostles, to bind Jews and Gentiles together in one body in Christ. If you have a *Trinity Hymnal*, meditate on the words of the hymn entitled "For All the Saints" (358 in the red hymnal; 281 in the blue). Ask God to use you more effectively in your local body of believers and to deepen your love for all the saints throughout the world.

3. Paul's conversion marked a 180-degree turn in his life. All of the energy, passion, zeal, and skill he had previously committed to furthering Pharisaic Judaism was immediately redirected to the cause of Christ. Paul's personality, ability, and talents did not change, but his focus did. One moment he was going full steam in one direction; the next moment he was going full steam in the opposite direction. Not everyone's conversion experience resembles Paul's. Many

people "grow up into faith" as they are raised in Christian homes. But many of us can pinpoint a specific moment in time when we stopped dead in our tracks, turned away from our sinful pursuits, and turned to Christ in faith.

If your conversion experience resembled Paul's in this way, evaluate how closely your *post-conversion* experience resembles his. To what did you devote the majority of your energy and skill before you were converted? How passionate and zealous were you in these pursuits? Do you now devote as much of your energy and skill to spiritual pursuits? Are you as passionate and zealous about these spiritual pursuits as you were about your pre-conversion pursuits? In answering these questions, keep in mind that you may be doing many of the same things (rearing children, making a home, running a business, working in an office, encouraging others, participating in community affairs) but with a different focus and purpose in mind. The same activity may be either a worldly or a spiritual pursuit, depending upon whether you are doing it with self-centered or God-centered motives. How does Paul's example convict and encourage you to intensify your commitment to spiritual pursuits? List several specific ways you might imitate Paul's walk with the Lord. Then make a plan to help you implement these ways of imitating him.

If your conversion experience was not sudden, like Paul's, evaluate your growth in faith over the years. Do you see an increasing pattern of commitment to spiritual pursuits? A decreasing pattern? A mixed pattern? How does Paul's example convict and encourage you to pursue spiritual commitment more faithfully in the future? Make a plan that will help you imitate Paul's walk with the Lord.

4. Paul went to great lengths to establish his apostolic authority in order to counter the false teaching of the Judaizers in Galatia. None of us is a Christ-appointed apostle like Paul. Does that mean we should not counter the false teaching we hear in our day and age? Does it mean we cannot speak truth authoritatively? Explain. Support your answers to these questions with Scripture, and illustrate them with examples from your personal life or from current affairs in our culture.

## Digging Deeper

1. Read Acts 16:1–5; 1 Corinthians 9:19–23; and Galatians 2:1–10. Explain Paul's reasons for circumcising Timothy and refusing to circumcise Titus. Then explain how his actions are completely consistent with his proclamation of the gospel.

2. Genesis 6:1–22; 2 Kings 11:1–21; and the Gospel accounts of the apostles' desertion of Jesus on the night of his death are three examples of times when God's divine plan seemed to teeter on the brink of extinction—and yet did not fail. Can you think of others? Study these examples and describe what you learn about God's sovereignty.

*Primary Passage*
GALATIANS 2:11–21

*Supplementary Passages*
GENESIS 12:3
LEVITICUS 18:5
PROVERBS 29:25
JEREMIAH 31:31–34
EZEKIEL 11:19–20; 36:22–27
ACTS 9:32–11:18; 13:38–39; 15:22–29
ROMANS 3:21–5:2; 6:14; 8:1–4
1 CORINTHIANS 10:12–13
2 CORINTHIANS 5:17
EPHESIANS 2:11–22
COLOSSIANS 2:11–15, 20–23
1 TIMOTHY 5:17–22
JAMES 2:8–13

Before reading the lesson material, please read the primary Scripture passage listed above and as many of the supplementary passages as time allows. Then briefly summarize in your notebook what you have read. (Do not go into detail. Limit your summary to a brief description of the people, events, and/or ideas discussed in the passages.)

# Only One Way of Being Christian

*How often our message and our methods in Christian service are dictated by the reactions (real or imagined) of others! As a result, the gospel waters are muddied, their clarity lost, their sparkle diminished, their taste compromised. If needy souls are to be refreshed, we must lead them to the pristine springs of grace in Christ, and that we shall do if we proclaim that grace fearlessly.* —EDGAR H. ANDREWS

One of the most difficult skills new writers must learn and seasoned writers must hone is the delicate art of

transition. Moving smoothly from one topic, point, or idea to another is extremely difficult, particularly when the connection between them is less than obvious to the average reader.

When I first started writing, Thom Notaro at P&R Publishing gently showed me my tendency to make connections in my head without bothering to inform my readers how I had moved from "point A" to "point B." Much of what I wrote made good sense to me, some sense to Thom, but little sense to anyone else. Thom has helped me get better at letting my readers connect the dots with me, but I know there is still room for improvement. So I make it a point to study the work of writers who do transition well.

One of those writers is the apostle Paul. Galatians 2:11–21 is one of the finest examples of well-done transition that I have ever read. In fact, I got so wrapped up in examining Paul's technique that I had to remind myself more than once to pay attention to what he was saying!

You should recall that Paul wrote Galatians to counter the first century's most serious threat to the gospel of grace. The brand of legalism being marketed by Judaizers to the folks in Galatia targeted three aspects of Christianity's essence: apostolic authority, justification, and sanctification. Paul's letter rebuts their false doctrine and proclaims God's truth regarding each of those points.

Paul defends the first point, his apostolic authority to speak truth from God, in Galatians 1:10–2:14. In our last lesson (covering 1:10–2:10), we saw him establish his apostolic independence from and harmony with the other Christ-appointed apostles. As we examine Galatians 2:11–14 in this lesson, we will see him assert his apostolic right to rebuke Peter, the most prestigious of those Christ-appointed apostles. Then, while describing the nature of his rebuke of Peter (2:15–21), he will glide effortlessly into the second point of his letter: the nature of justification. Take it from someone who is still learning the fine art of transition: Galatians 2:11–21 is a masterpiece.

## Opposing Peter

### *(Galatians 2:11–14)*

To set up his masterful transition verses, Paul recalls a confrontation between himself and Peter.[1]

> But when Cephas came to Antioch, I opposed him to his face, because he stood condemned. For prior to the coming of certain men from James, he used to eat with the Gentiles; but when they came, he began to withdraw and hold himself aloof, fearing the party of the circumcision. The rest of the Jews joined him in hypocrisy, with the result that even Barnabas was carried away by their hypocrisy. But when I saw that they were not straightforward about the truth of the gospel, I said to Cephas in the presence of all, "If you, being a Jew, live like the Gentiles and not like the Jews, how is it that you compel the Gentiles to live like Jews?" (2:11–14)

Why did Paul repeat this story to the Galatians? Did he desire to humiliate Peter or exalt himself above the other apostles? No. Scripture reveals Paul to be neither vengeful nor arrogant. His motives for telling the Galatians about his confrontation with Peter were altogether righteous and entirely appropriate. He did it for at least three very good reasons: (1) to establish his apostolic authority as equal to Peter's, (2) to emphasize the power of influence, and (3) to highlight the ease with which even mature Christians fall into hypocrisy.[2]

Peter was "first among equals"[3] within the band of Christ-appointed apostles, a leader of leaders, the point-man in Jewish evangelism, respected, influential, and greatly admired. He was "the rock," a strong part of the foundation upon which Jesus built His church in the world (Ephesians 2:20). He held "the keys of the Kingdom" and had been authorized to bind and loose on earth what God had bound and loosed in heaven (Matthew 16:13–19).

Peter was a man few people would dare "oppose to his face." It took a man of equal standing before God and the church to stand nose to nose with "the rock" and charge him with hypocrisy. The fact that Paul had done it with evident success validated his claim of apostolic authority and enhanced his credibility in combating the Judaizers.

But that is not the only end served by the story. Telling the Galatians *why* he had confronted Peter was, in effect, a veiled but firm exhortation for those who think they stand to take heed lest they fall. If a man of Peter's standing and godliness could fall prey to hypocrisy and lead others astray, so can the rest of us. Peter succumbed to hypocrisy because he had a weakness for people-pleasing[4]—a weakness with which most of us readily identify.

Paul explained that prior to the coming of "certain men from James," Peter customarily ate with Gentiles. He had, after all, received a triple-vision from God telling him that the old dividing wall between Jew and Gentile had been demolished and that a new basis for distinctively Christian fellowship had been erected in its place. Believers in Jesus Christ were now *united in Him* by the outpouring of His Holy Spirit. Their union was no longer grounded in the shared observance of Jewish rituals (Acts 10:1–11:18). Peter had faithfully preached this new basis for fellowship and consistently lived out what he preached—until "the James Gang"[5] showed up in Antioch. Then he began "to withdraw and hold himself aloof" because he feared the party of the circumcision.

What was it about those fellows from James that caused Peter the Rock to crack and crumble? We cannot be sure because Paul did not tell us. But we can speculate. Perhaps they told him that his "brotherly" conduct with Gentiles would be a stumbling block to the very Jews he was working so hard to evangelize. Maybe they hinted that his fraternization with Gentile sinners might actually spark greater dissension within the church. They might have criticized him or insulted him or threatened to ruin his reputation. They could have simply watched his every move and made copious notes.

Frankly, I would love to know what they said or did that shook Peter up. But Paul chose to skip that part of the story. He said only that Peter feared them and began to withdraw from his Gentile brothers and sisters. John MacArthur dubs it a "sneaky retreat."[6] Peter did not stand up and announce to the church that his understanding of the gospel had changed and therefore he had to quit eating with Gentiles. In fact, we have no reason to think his beliefs about the basis of Christian fellowship had changed in the slightest. But Scripture is clear that his behavior surely had.

Peter put on the mask of hypocrisy. He became a "two-faced" Christian—acting contrary to his professed beliefs. And because he was a significant leader, his behavior had a significant impact on others. Paul said the rest of the Jews joined him in hypocrisy. Even Barnabas, Paul's loyal friend and a man known for his great gifts of encouragement and mediation, followed in Peter's wayward footsteps.

Of course, we do not have to be a pillar like Peter for our behavior to have a great impact on others. Regardless of how insignificant we may think we are, all kinds of people are watching us live. Many of them use us as guides for their own behavior. Maybe they shouldn't. Maybe we wish they wouldn't. Maybe we even tell them not to. But the fact is, they do. All of us influence the people around us with our words, our attitudes, and our actions. Peter's example should cause us to stop and think about who looks to us as models of "Christianity in the flesh," and to realize that growth in Christlikeness is as important for evangelism and discipling as it is for our own sanctification.

Peter's example should also cause us to realize that the more high-profile a life, the greater the impact its words, attitudes, and behavior will have. A well-known pastor-teacher with an international ministry once told a story of a man who approached him in the baggage claim area of an airport. After acknowledging that he had recognized the pastor during the flight and telling how much he appreciated his ministry, the man said, "I was watching you on that airplane to see how you treated the flight attendants and what you were reading and what you were drinking. I just wanted to know whether you live what you preach." The pastor-teacher confessed to not fully realizing the importance of living out what he preached until that very moment. It suddenly became very clear that the credibility of his message depended in large part on the credibility of his life.

The credibility of Peter's message took a nosedive when his life ceased to reflect the truths that he preached. And the credibility of Peter's message was Paul's primary concern. He told

Peter point-blank that his weakness for people-pleasing had implications that ran deeper than fellowship issues. Refusing to eat with his Gentile brethren actually decried the truth of the gospel he preached. Although Peter *said* that justification was by grace through faith in Christ, his behavior said justification was by faith plus works. Paul confronted him with the fact that rebuilding the dividing wall God had demolished was nothing less than a denial of the gospel of grace.

Timothy George explains that the controversy in Antioch was much more than a clash between two apostles. It was a collision between two ways of being Christian.[7] Paul confronted Peter "in the presence of all" because his influential hypocrisy threatened the spread of the only *God-revealed* way of being Christian. And he told the Galatians the story because the influential deception of Judaizers was doing the very same thing.

## Being Christian

### *(Galatians 2:15–21)*

So what is the only God-revealed way of being Christian? Paul reminded Peter and the Galatians[8] that it was not by being Jewish. Being Jewish had a lot to do with observing the law. In fact, the privilege of having the law to observe was perhaps the greatest benefit of being Jewish. James Buchanan explains that the law was given to the Jewish people, at the time God formed them into a nation, for their instruction in relating to God and to each other and also to prepare them, by a course of discipline and education, for the coming of Christ.[9]

The law reflected God's character to His chosen people and laid down His righteous requirements of them in written codes. It defined godly morality, provided a means of recognizing and dealing with sin, and structured God-honoring lifestyles. It even held out a promise of eternal life in return for perfect obedience (Leviticus 18:5).

But beneficial as the law was for Jews, it could not save them. That is because all Jews were fallen sinners and therefore unable to obey the law perfectly. Salvation for Jews came through having faith in God's promise of a Messiah-Redeemer who would keep the law perfectly and atone for their sin. This promise was first made to Abraham long before the law was given to Moses.

The law clarified the need for the Messiah-Redeemer by impressing upon the Jews (1) God's holiness, righteousness, and justice, (2) the extent of the obedience they owed to God, (3) the number and heinousness of their sins, and (4) their utter inability to escape the wrath of God aside from taking refuge in His gracious promise.[10]

For Jews, observing the law was a means of acknowledging their helpless condition and expressing faith in God's promise. When Jews kept the law *as an expression of repentance and faith*, they testified of their right standing with God. People are made right with God when they are counted righteous in His sight and forgiven for their transgressions against Him. The law pictured the only means by which they could be forgiven and counted righteous: the work of the Messiah-Redeemer who would do for them what they could not do for themselves (Acts 13:38–39).

God's choice of Israel to receive the promise and the law erected a temporary dividing wall between Israel and all other nations. Since being made right with God required faith in the promise expressed through observance of the law, Gentiles could come to God only through Judaism. But when the

Messiah-Redeemer appeared, the promise was fulfilled and the dividing wall fell. Jesus Christ fulfilled God's promise to bless all the nations through Abraham (Genesis 12:3). He lived on this earth in perfect obedience to all of God's law. He died on the cross to fully satisfy God's wrath against our sin so that we could be forgiven. His life and death met every requirement of the law *on behalf of* those from *all nations* whom God had chosen to save.

God declared Christ's work acceptable when He raised Him from the dead and installed Him in the position of authority at His right hand. People of all nations are now made right with God when they exercise God-given faith (that is, when they believe and trust) in what Jesus has done. Exercising that faith *unites* us with Him and *gives* us the righteousness and forgiveness we need to be made right with God. We stand before God *in Christ*, clothed in His righteousness and forgiven on the basis of His atonement. Faith alone in the *completed work* of Christ is now the way in which people from all nations are made right with God. That's why being Christian isn't about being Jewish.

Paul knew that. And so did Peter. But Peter had a weakness for people-pleasing. He caved in to Jews who were desperately trying to preserve their identity by casting Christianity in a Jewish mold. Paul knew that such efforts effectively denied what Christ had done and if allowed to persist would destroy the faith. So he exhorted Peter with a pointed reminder that neither of them had been "justified" (made right with God) by works of the law but by faith in Christ.

> We are Jews by nature and not sinners from among the Gentiles; nevertheless knowing that a man is not justified by the works of

the Law but through faith in Christ Jesus, even we have believed in Christ Jesus, so that we may be justified by faith in Christ and not by the works of the Law; since by the works of the Law no flesh will be justified. (Galatians 2:15–16)

Historically, Jews defined Gentiles as "sinners" simply because they were Gentiles. Although Jews also sinned, they had the means of recognizing and dealing with their sin by observing the provisions of the law that pictured the coming work of Christ. Gentiles were "sinners" because they had no comparable means of being made right with God. But the coming of Christ had leveled the playing field. Now, Jew and Gentile alike were made right with God through faith in Christ.

Paul's bold affirmation that salvation is through faith, not works, obviously stirred up persistent opposition from Jews who believed that "no law" meant "no holiness." Detractors probably dogged Paul's steps and rebutted his teaching by shouting: "Don't listen to Paul! He teaches that Jesus Christ did away with the law and opened the door for Jew and Gentile to sin freely without consequence." Paul was so accustomed to their attacks that his letters usually anticipated and countered would-be objectors. His letter to the Galatians is no exception. Before he launched into an extended explanation of why faith in Christ cannot coexist with "works of the Law," he addressed a few words to his opponents:

But if, while seeking to be justified in Christ, we ourselves have also been found sinners, is Christ then a minister of sin? May it never be! For if I rebuild what I have once destroyed, I prove myself to be a transgressor. For through the Law I died to the Law, so that I might live to God. I have been crucified with Christ; and it is no longer I who live, but Christ lives in me;

and the life which I now live in the flesh I live by faith in the Son of God, who loved me and gave Himself up for me. I do not nullify the grace of God, for if righteousness comes through the Law, then Christ died needlessly. (2:17–21)

Paul denounced his opponents' arguments as absolutely ridiculous. Jesus Christ did not live and die on this earth in order to substitute a "license of faith" for the "righteousness of the Law." His life and death replaced external constraint that demanded holiness but lacked internal transformation that generates both desire and ability for holy living.

The law defines righteousness and reveals our sinfulness. And then it points us to Christ as the solution for sinfulness. That is why Paul said "through the Law" he "died to the Law" so that he could "live to God." The law convicts us, but it cannot equip us to freely obey. It can constrain our behavior, but it cannot transform our desires. It cannot give us the righteousness that most glorifies God.

The righteousness that most glorifies God does not come from restrictive rule-keeping; it comes from regenerated delight in pursuing Christlikeness. The righteousness that most glorifies God is about spiritual new birth. It reflects His power at work in His people. It is born when our hard hearts of stone are replaced with soft hearts of flesh. And it matures in the strength of His indwelling Spirit. The righteousness that most glorifies God is not something we *have* to do in order to stay on His good side. It is something we *get* to do because we have been saved and transformed for the purpose of giving Him glory.

Justification *unites us* with Christ. And union with Christ makes us new creations—free from the external constraint of the law, motivated by the internal principle of holiness, and empowered by God's Spirit to pursue the righteousness that most glorifies God. John Calvin explains that our union with Christ frees us to "live the life of God" instead of living to gain His approval. God's gracious provision of acceptance in Christ assures us of His approval and gives us a new energy and "life force" that frees us to live a completely different kind and quality of life. We are liberated from the guilt and curse of the law and empowered by the indwelling Holy Spirit to live as new creations instead of striving to meet a standard of approval.[11] John MacArthur captures Calvin's idea well when he says, "The Christian life is not so much a believer living for Christ as Christ's living through the believer."[12]

Paul testified to what union with Christ had meant for him. It meant dying to his agenda, his work, and his abilities. And it meant being reborn to live out Christ's agenda because of Christ's work in the power of Christ's abilities. The faith that fueled that kind of life had not wiped righteousness out of Paul's life. On the contrary, it had stimulated and empowered him to live far more righteously than the law ever had.

Faith alone in Christ alone frees us to be righteous in ways that the law never could. The law merely pictured what Christ accomplished. Paul said that if law-keeping could give us enough righteousness to be made right with God, then Christ's life and death were utterly pointless.

## Notes

1.  Most commentators agree that we cannot know for certain when this visit took place. One intriguing possibility is that

Peter went to Antioch when he fled Jerusalem following a miraculous escape from prison (Acts 12:1–17).

2. The word "hypocrisy" originated in the Greek theater where the actors wore masks. It has come to mean pretense, insincerity, or acting in a manner that gives a false notion of true intent or belief.

3. Many commentators use this term to emphasize Peter's distinctive leadership calling, which gave him a unique position among the apostles but did not make him "better" than they.

4. Although Peter proudly boasted that he would never deny his Lord (Matthew 26:35; Luke 22:33), he was intimidated into doing so by strangers in a crowd (Matthew 26:69–75; Mark 14:66–72; Luke 22:54–62).

5. I borrowed this delightfully descriptive phrase from Philip Graham Ryken, *Galatians*, Reformed Expository Commentary (Phillipsburg, N.J.: P&R Publishing, 2005), 60.

6. John MacArthur Jr., *Galatians*, The MacArthur New Testament Commentary (Chicago: Moody Press, 1987), 57.

7. Timothy George, *An Exegetical and Theological Exposition of Galatians*, The New American Commentary (Nashville: Broadman and Holman, 1994), 172.

8. All the commentators I have read agree that it is impossible to tell where Paul's quoted remarks to Peter end and his explanation of those remarks to the Galatians begin in this passage.

9. James Buchanan, *The Doctrine of Justification* (1867; reprint, Carlisle, Pa.: Banner of Truth, 1961), 37.

10. Ibid, 38.

11. John Calvin, *Commentaries on the Epistles of Paul to the Galatians and Ephesians*, trans. William Pringle (reprint, Grand Rapids, Mich.: Baker, 2003), 73–74.

12. MacArthur, *Galatians*, 60.

## E X E R C I S E S

### REVIEW

1. In Galatians 1:10–2:14, Paul offers three distinct points that affirm his apostolic authority to speak from God. Describe these three points and explain how each affirms his apostolic authority.

2. What purposes were served by Paul's telling the Galatians about his confrontation with Peter at Antioch?

3. What aspects of Peter's behavior in Antioch made it hypocritical? What was Paul's primary concern regarding Peter's hypocrisy?

4. Describe the importance of the law to the Jews.

5. How are people made right with God?

6. How did the coming of Christ change the way in which God's chosen people relate to the law?

   Note: If answering Review exercises 4–6 is difficult for you, do not despair. Paul's teaching in these areas is expanded and clarified in Galatians 3–4.

7. Does faith in Christ apart from "works of the Law" eliminate the need for holiness in the life of a believer? Explain your answer emphasizing the significance of the believer's union with Christ.

## APPLICATION

1. This week review previous memory verses and begin memorizing one or more of the following Scripture passages:

   Romans 3:21–26

   1 Corinthians 10:12–13

   Galatians 2:20

2. This week in your prayer time, use Ezekiel 11:19–20; 36:22–27; and 2 Corinthians 5:17 to help you thank God for transforming your heart and making you a new creation in Christ. Ask Him to reveal specific areas of your life in which you are not living consistently with what you profess to believe, and to help you make changes in your thoughts, attitudes, and behavior that will reflect His glory more.

3. John Calvin said that our union with Christ frees us to "live the life of God" instead of living to gain His approval. John MacArthur said essentially the same thing: "The Christian life is not so much a believer living for Christ as Christ's living through the believer." Consider the distinction these men are making. What thoughts, attitudes, and behaviors characterize a person who "lives the life of God" (the person *through whom* Christ lives)? What thoughts, attitudes, and behaviors characterize a person who lives to gain God's approval (who lives *for* Christ)? What is the difference between living to gain God's approval and living to reflect God's glory? How does rightly understanding justification (being made right with God through what *Christ* has done) clarify the dis-

tinction these men are making? Why is the distinction they are making important?

Now consider how the distinction they are making applies to you. Has this lesson helped you understand justification well enough to see the difference between living to gain God's approval and living to reflect His glory? If so, thank God for this insight and ask God in prayer to help you "live the life of God" more consistently. If not, prayerfully seek additional input from other resources regarding the nature of justification (several good resources are listed in the Recommended Reading section at the end of this book). Please do not shrug this distinction off as a "fine theological point" that is largely irrelevant for Christian living. Walking worthy of your high calling in Christ amounts to *living out* a right understanding of how justification unites you with Christ and transforms your heart.

## DIGGING DEEPER

Suppose a friend of yours has just called and told you that she was listening to the radio on the way home from the mall and heard part of a sermon on Galatians being preached by Philip Graham Ryken. She is thoroughly confused by this statement: "If we can be saved by our own works, then Jesus was a false Messiah who died a worthless death on a meaningless cross" (Philip Graham Ryken, *Galatians*, Reformed Expository Commentary [Phillipsburg, N.J.: P&R Publishing, 2005], 77).

"I don't understand," she tells you. "Aren't we supposed to work out our salvation? Didn't God prepare good works for us to do before time began? Won't God say, 'Well done, good and faithful servant' if we do those good works? So, how can doing good works make Jesus a false Messiah whose death was meaningless?" Drawing on what you have learned in this lesson, write a paragraph or two that will help your friend understand what Pastor Ryken meant.

### Primary Passage
GALATIANS 3:1–9

### Supplementary Passages
GENESIS 12:3; 15:1–21; 17:1–14; 22:1–19
JEREMIAH 31:31–34
EZEKIEL 11:19–20; 36:22–28
MATTHEW 3:7–10; 8:5–12
LUKE 3:7–9; 12:32; 19:1–10
JOHN 8:39–40, 56
ACTS 15:13–18
ROMANS 4:1–25
1 CORINTHIANS 2:6–16
2 CORINTHIANS 3:4–18 ; 10:3–5
EPHESIANS 4:11–16
PHILIPPIANS 1:6
COLOSSIANS 2:6–15
HEBREWS 7:11–22; 11:8–19

Before reading the lesson material, please read the primary Scripture passage listed above and as many of the supplementary passages as time allows. Then briefly summarize in your notebook what you have read. (Do not go into detail. Limit your summary to a brief description of the people, events, and/or ideas discussed in the passages.)

# What Were You Thinking?

*The gospel of Christ crucified, as Paul saw it, so completely ruled out the law as a means of getting right with God that it was scarcely credible that people who had once embraced such a gospel should ever turn back to the law for salvation.*
—F. F. BRUCE

As I was growing up, my parents asked me a lot of questions. Not all those questions served the same purpose. Some were simple requests for information: "What time does the basketball game start tonight?" "Do you want bologna or chicken salad in your sandwich today?" Some were clearly polite commands: "Would you please take out the garbage?" "Can you answer the phone?" Some took the form of not-so-subtle reminders: "Did you finish your homework?" "Whose turn is it to do the dishes?" Some were little more than thinly veiled warnings: "Do you know what the speed limit is on this street? Do you want to end up like Aunt Thelma?" And some weren't really questions at all.

When I heard my parents say such things as "What on earth were you thinking?" "Have you lost your senses?" "How many times have I told you . . . ?" and "Who do you think you are?" I knew they were not actually *asking* me anything. Instead, they were expressing amazement that I, their beloved child who had had all the benefits of being so well cared for and wisely reared, could have done something so profoundly illogical and inconceivably contrary to my upbringing and maturity level.

Those kinds of questions are called "rhetorical" because they are not queries so much as "point makers." When my parents used them, they did not want me to answer their questions directly. (To do so would have gotten me into even more trouble.) Rather, they wanted me to concede their point that I had behaved foolishly. They wanted me to acknowledge that what I had done was glaringly inconsistent with sound reasoning, sensible living, their wise instruction, and my own identity.

Paul used rhetorical questions much as my parents did. In Galatians 3:1–5, he peppered his readers with six stinging questions that are not really questions at all. He did not expect the Galatians to answer his questions directly. Instead, he wanted them to concede his point that they were acting foolishly. He wanted them to acknowledge the utter absurdity of *experiencing* the true gospel of grace and then swallowing the false teaching of the Judaizers hook, line, and sinker.

Paul's sizzling set of pseudo-questions threw down a gauntlet the Galatians could not pick up. The *heteros* gospel they had gullibly guzzled bore no resemblance to what God had done in their lives. The gospel that saved them was the very same gospel that had saved God's chosen saints within the nation of Israel. All had been saved by God-given faith in the work of Christ Jesus.[1] Paul had taught the Galatians that truth. They had experienced that truth. And yet they had believed a lie that contradicted that truth.

Although Paul was appalled at the ease with which they had been duped, he loved them enough to rebuke and correct them. Having established his apostolic authority to speak for God, he devoted the rest of his letter to exposing their folly and correcting their thinking. He began with six "unanswerable" questions designed to force them to face facts. The doctrine of Judaizers bore no resemblance to their own experience of God's saving grace and enabling power.

## What Saved You, Galatians?

### (Galatians 3:1–5)

My parents had an arsenal of unanswerable questions, but "What were you thinking?" was clearly their favorite. They fired it when I needed to realize that my thought processes had fallen far short of my potential. They knew I was capable of thinking well but often neglected to make the effort. And they loved me too much to let me get by with it.

Paul fired his first question at the Galatians for the very same purpose. He had their best interests at heart when he wrote, "You foolish Galatians, who has bewitched you, before whose eyes Jesus Christ was publicly portrayed as crucified?" (3:1). He knew they were capable of thinking much more clearly than they were. So he urged them to think better by highlighting the foolishness of their behavior. He chose the Greek word *anoētos* rather than *mōros* to describe them not as mentally lacking but as mentally lax.

They had been "bewitched"—enchanted, fascinated, led astray, duped, and deceived—not because they were stupid or ignorant people, but because they were lazy and careless thinkers. Edgar Andrews says they failed "to apply their faith-enlightened minds to discern truth from error."[2] They allowed themselves to be carried about by every wind of doctrine. They surrendered to hollow philosophy and empty deception. They opened themselves up to the traditions of men. All because they failed to take every thought captive to the obedience of Christ.

Paul reminded them that there was no reasonable excuse for their mental sloth. Before their very eyes, Jesus Christ had been "publicly portrayed as crucified." The phrase "publicly portrayed" calls up images of wanted posters in the local post office or "for rent" notices on the bulletin board at the Laundromat. Paul had placarded the gospel in public for all to see and hear. He had posted the good news that the redemption of sinners was finished and complete in the crucifixion of Christ. He had announced that the cross left no gap between God and His elect that had to be bridged by human works. He had proclaimed that, on the cross, Jesus Christ *accomplished* salvation by fulfilling all of God's righteous requirements and absorbing all of His righteous wrath against the sin of those God would save. Paul pointed to the cross as proof that God's chosen people had been, finally and absolutely, made right with Him.

Paul's first rhetorical question fairly resonates with the implications of such a gospel. How could a *finished* gospel come with human merit attached? How could a *completed* gospel be contingent on ceremonies? Paul wanted his readers to see that supplementing Christ's work supplants what He has done.[3] He wanted them to recall that the only way to receive the gospel he preached was by hearing with faith.

How could the Galatians have understood Paul's gospel well enough to be saved by it and then "so quickly" have swallowed the false teaching of the Judaizers? Simply put, they were thinking well below their ability. They were embracing beliefs that were out of touch with reality—beliefs that denied what God had done in their lives. Paul was understandably irked at their mental malingering—and wasn't about to let them get by with it. Thinly veiled irritation permeated irresistible logic as Paul made the point they needed to concede: their own experience verified that Christianity is lived out the same way it began—in the power of God's Holy Spirit received by grace through hearing with faith. Believing doctrine that contradicted their own experience was nothing short of ridiculous.

Study Paul's argument carefully and see if you can follow the flow of his reasoning.

This is the only thing I want to find out from you: did you receive the Spirit by the works of the Law, or by hearing with faith? Are you so foolish? Having begun by the Spirit, are you now being perfected by the flesh? Did you suffer so many things in vain—if indeed it was in vain? So then, does He who provides you with the Spirit and works miracles among you, do it by the works of the Law, or by hearing with faith? (3:2–5)

Did you appreciate the skill with which Paul wrote those questions? Did you observe that their wording and organization make his point irrefutably? Did you see that a correct answer to the first question determines the answers to all the others? Did you detect the progression *from* their initial experience of salvation *through* their experience of Christian living *to* Paul's conclusion that being Christian, from start to finish, is God's work in us, not our work for Him?

If so, put another gold star on the title page of your book. If not, read the passage again with my questions in mind. Then rejoin us as we think through Paul's brilliant logic together. He begins by setting a baited trap in his readers' path. "I just want to know one thing, Galatians," he says in essence. "How were you saved? Did you receive God's indwelling Spirit as a reward for meritorious conduct? Or as a free gift of God's grace?" The answer was patently obvious.

Most of those reading Paul's letter were Gentiles. They could not have received the Spirit by works of the law because they did not know God's law existed until *after* they were saved. They knew very well when they had received the Holy Spirit—at the moment they heard and believed the gospel about Jesus Christ. When they put their trust in what Christ had done for them, God saved them and sent His Spirit to live in them. They had indeed received the Spirit "by hearing with faith," not "by the works of the Law."

God's indwelling Spirit was a gift that equipped them to live for God's glory. And the Giver expected them to use it for that purpose. They had been saved to do good works that glorify God (Matthew 5:16; Ephesians 2:10); and good works that glorify God are empowered by His Holy Spirit (1 Corinthians 10:31; 2 Corinthians 4:7). Paul emphasized how foolish they were to think they could begin "by the Spirit" and be "perfected by the flesh." Flesh-powered living does not glorify God; only Spirit-powered obedience gives God the glory He so richly deserves (2 Corinthians 3:5–6; Philippians 4:13).

Paul implies that they *had* experienced the Spirit's enabling power when he asked incredulously, "Did you suffer so many things in vain—if indeed it was in vain?" The Greek word translated "suffer" can refer to life experiences in general as well as to difficulties and trials. And there is no general consensus among commentators as to how Paul intended it to be understood. Fortunately, his point is clear regardless of which way we translate it.

The Galatians knew firsthand the life-changing power of Christian conversion. They had been transformed (changed, reconstructed, rewired) to serve a new purpose. They had become new creations whose renewed minds were set on the things above, not the things of this world. Their hard hearts of stone had been converted into soft hearts of flesh that desired to forsake sin and serve God. They had watched God work in and through them far more abundantly beyond all they could ask or think, according to the power that worked within them (Ephesians 3:20).

How could they ignore or deny the clear evidence of God's working mightily in their daily lives? Only if they were not thinking as well as they could. If they followed Paul's well-reasoned appeal to their own experience, they would have to concede his foregone conclusion: "He who provides you with the Spirit and works miracles among you" does it "by hearing with faith," not "by the works of the Law."

Paul's impeccable logic left them no choice but to admit that the doctrine of the Judaizers was not what had saved them.

But Paul's case does not rest solely on what had happened to the Galatians. He goes on to show that the doctrine of the Judaizers had never saved anyone.

## What Saved Father Abraham?

### *(Galatians 3:6–9)*

Paul was not saying that the doctrine of the Judaizers was simply old-fashioned, outdated, or behind the times. Nor was he saying that its proponents were merely stuck in past centuries and resistant to change. Nor was he accusing them of holding on to the old tried-and-true Jewish gospel in protest against his new-and-improved Gentile gospel. Paul did not "take on" the Judaizers because their doctrine was obsolete; he took them on because their doctrine was wrong. His point was not that "works of the Law" *no longer* saved, but that they had *never* saved.

He began at the beginning with Father Abraham, who, according to Scripture, was saved just as were the Galatians—by hearing with faith, not by works of the law.

> Even so Abraham believed God, and it was reckoned to him as righteousness. Therefore, be sure that it is those who are of faith who are sons of Abraham. The Scripture, foreseeing that God would justify the Gentiles by faith, preached the gospel beforehand to Abraham, saying, "All the nations will be blessed in you." So then those who are of faith are blessed with Abraham, the believer. (3:6–9)

Like so many effective debaters, Paul launched his argument from a point of agreement. Both he and the Judaizers believed that Abraham's salvation served as the pattern for everyone else's. However, they parted company on the issue of how he was saved. The Judaizers taught that Abraham's obedience to God's commands made him right with God. They opened their scrolls to Genesis 17 and read the account of God's great promises to Abraham followed by this clear command: "Now as for you, you shall keep My covenant, you and your descendants after you throughout their generations. This is My covenant, which you shall keep, between Me and you and your descendants after you: every male among you shall be circumcised" (vv. 9–10).

*There you have it,* they may well have concluded. *Abraham's participation in God's covenant (which included the promise of salvation through the coming Messiah) depended upon his being circumcised. God accepted him and all of his natural descendants because they obeyed this covenant commandment. Obviously, circumcision is a must if you want to participate in the blessings of God's covenant—and that goes for Gentiles as well as for Jews.*

Paul countered by charging them with the egregious exegetical error of context abuse. They had missed the point of this significant event in Abraham's life because they ignored equally significant *previous* events in his life. Paul rolled his scroll back to Genesis 15 and read this account:

. . . the word of the LORD came to Abram in a vision, saying,

"Do not fear, Abram,
I am a shield to you;
Your reward shall be very great."

Abram said, "O Lord GOD, what will You give me, since I am childless, and the heir of my house is Eliezer of Damascus?" . . .

Then behold, the word of the LORD came to him, saying, "This man will not be your heir; but one who will come forth from your own body, he shall be your heir." And He took him outside and said, "Now look toward the heavens, and count the stars, if you are able to count them. . . . So shall your descendants be." (vv. 1–5)

From a human standpoint, God's words were incredible—impossible to believe. Even so, Abraham heard God with faith. Scripture testifies that Abraham "believed God, and it was reckoned to him as righteousness" (Galatians 3:6). The word translated "reckoned" means credited, put to one's account, placed on deposit. Abraham's belief, his hearing with faith, was credited to him as righteousness. Paul argued indisputably that Abraham was made right with God when he believed in God's promise—long before he obeyed God's command to be circumcised.

At the time Abraham was counted righteous, God also illustrated the nature of their covenantal relationship. He told Abraham to collect "a three year old heifer, and a three year old female goat, and a three year old ram, and a turtledove, and a young pigeon" (Genesis 15:9). These Abraham cut in two (except for the birds) and "laid each half opposite the other" (v. 10). Then he spent the rest of the day chasing away birds of prey. At nightfall, he fell into a deep, troubled sleep. While he slept, God, in the form of a smoking oven and a flaming torch, passed *alone* through the cut animals (vv. 12–17). These events signified that although Abraham and his descendants would have covenant responsibilities to perform, fulfillment of the covenant promises depended on God's Word alone.

Thus Paul put circumcision in its proper place. It was a covenant responsibility designed to identify God's chosen people as distinctly His own. Obedience marked Israel as a nation separated to God, but did not make any individual Jew right with God. Any Jew who enjoyed right standing with God did so through hearing with faith, not by works of the law.

And that went for Gentiles as well as for Jews. Gentile salvation was no "divine afterthought." Scripture teaches that God had always intended to "justify the Gentiles by faith." God Himself preached this gospel to Abraham in Genesis 12 when He said, "In you all the families of the earth will be blessed" (v. 3). *All* who shared Abraham's faith would share in the blessing of right standing with God.

The Galatians to whom Paul wrote had heard and believed. They had been saved solely by faith, but had then fallen prey to the false teaching of legalism. As we noted earlier, they were bewitched (enchanted and deceived), not because they were stupid or ignorant people, but because they were lazy and careless thinkers. Paul loved them too much to let them get by with it and urgently wrote to rebuke and correct them. God inspired what Paul wrote and made sure his letter ended up in our Bible. He knew Christians down through the ages would need Paul's instruction just as much as the Galatians did. We also are prone to fall for false doctrine because we fail to think as well as we can.

As we study the rest of Galatians, Paul's words to our first-century brethren will rebuke and correct us as well. He will challenge us to think long and hard about God's revealed truth and to define our doctrine accordingly. His words will convict us, stretch us, and instruct us. They will drive most of us far out of our comfort zones and highlight our dependence on God's indwelling Spirit. But if we heed them, Paul's words will also equip us to walk worthy of our high calling in Christ. They will help us set our minds on the things above and seek first His kingdom and righteousness. They will make us more effective at giving God glory.

The remaining chapters of Galatians demand careful attention. So, roll up the sleeves of your mind and buckle down to think. We are about to engage in some strenuous mental exertion, but don't shrink back in fear. It will be effort well spent, and we will not regret it.

## Notes

1. Old Testament saints were saved by looking *forward* in faith to the work of Jesus Christ, whereas New Testament saints are saved by looking *back* in faith to His work.

2. Edgar H. Andrews, *Free in Christ: The Message of Galatians*, The Welwyn Commentary Series (Durham, England: Evangelical Press, 1996), 126.

3. This sentence is a paraphrase of William Hendriksen's statement, "A Christ supplemented is a Christ supplanted" (*New Testament Commentary: Galatians, Ephesians, Philippians, Colossians, and Philemon* [Grand Rapids, Mich.: Baker, 1996], 112).

### EXERCISES

#### REVIEW

1. What are rhetorical questions and why do people use them?

2. Explain the significance of Paul's choice of words (*anoētos* instead of *mōros*) to describe the Galatians as foolish.

3. What was so foolish about the Galatians' behavior?

4. Explain the progression of Paul's irresistible logic in Galatians 3:2–5. How does his logic soundly refute the teaching of the Judaizers?

5. Using evidence from the life of Abraham, support Paul's implication that the doctrine of the Judaizers had never saved anyone.

<u>APPLICATION</u>

1. This week review previous memory verses and begin memorizing one or more of the following Scripture passages:

   Romans 4:19–22

   Philippians 1:6

   Colossians 2:6–8

2. This week in your prayer time, use Romans 4:13–25 and 2 Corinthians 3:4–6 to help you thank God for saving you by grace and equipping you by grace to serve Him. Thank Him for your particular spiritual gifts and natural abilities and the opportunities He has provided for you to use them.

3. Read the following passages carefully: 1 Corinthians 2:6–16; 2 Corinthians 10:3–5; Ephesians 4:11–16; Colossians 2:6–15. Consult reliable commentaries, if necessary, to help you understand what you have read. Then describe how the truths contained in these passages relate to the situation in Galatia that prompted Paul's letter. Edgar Andrews states that the situation in first-century Galatia was not all that different from our own. He says that we

also are tempted (1) to forsake sound doctrine in favor of novelty or excitement, (2) to submit to human ideologies instead of God's truth, (3) to tailor the gospel to suit the tastes of men, (4) to compromise truth for the sake of peace, and (5) to neglect the hard work of thinking for ourselves and allow ourselves to be led around blindly by persuasive teachers (Edgar H. Andrews, *Free in Christ: The Message of Galatians*, The Welwyn Commentary Series [Durham, England: Evangelical Press, 1996], 126). Cite at least one specific twenty-first century example to illustrate each of Andrews's points. Stay close to home in your examples. Think about how you or your church or your family members have been tempted in these ways. Pray before you begin, asking the Lord to reveal sins that you need to confess and forsake. List several ways you can contribute to turning the tide of "Galatianism" in our culture, and make a specific step-by-step plan that will help you implement at least one of the items on your list immediately.

4. Which of Paul's six rhetorical questions convicted you most? Explain your answer and describe what actions you will take to correct the issues about which you were convicted.

DIGGING DEEPER

Timothy George says that Romans 4 is the best commentary on Galatians 3 (Timothy George, *An Exegetical and Theological Exposition of Galatians*, The New American Commentary [Nashville: Broadman and Holman, 1994], 219–20). Study Galatians 3 in light of Romans 4 and describe what you learn about faith from your study of these two chapters of Scripture. Consider, in particular, how faith relates to (1) boasting, (2) reason, and (3) obedience. In what ways did this study impact your thinking, attitudes, and behavior?

*Primary Passage*
GALATIANS 3:10–18

*Supplementary Passages*
GENESIS 3:15; 12:1–3; 15:1–21; 26:24–25; 28:10–17
LEVITICUS 18:1–5
DEUTERONOMY 21:22–23; 26:16–28:46; 30:19–20
JEREMIAH 31:31–34
EZEKIEL 11:19–20; 36:22–28
JOEL 2:28–29
HABAKKUK 1:12–13; 2:4
JOHN 3:36; 17:3
ACTS 13:38–39; 26:22–23
ROMANS 1:16–17; 3:19–26; 4:13–15; 5:1–21; 8:1–4, 14–17;
    10:1–4
1 CORINTHIANS 1:30–31; 15:56–57
2 CORINTHIANS 5:21
EPHESIANS 2:1–10
HEBREWS 10:1–18, 36–39
JAMES 2:10
1 PETER 1:17–21; 2:24
1 JOHN 3:1–10

Before reading the lesson material, please read the primary
Scripture passage listed above and as many of the supplementary passages as time allows. Then briefly summarize in
your notebook what you have read. (Do not go into detail.
Limit your summary to a brief description of the people,
events, and/or ideas discussed in the passages.)

# Diagnosis, Not Cure

*The curse is wrath revealed, and ruin threatened . . . and if, as
transgressors of the law, we are under the curse of it, it must be a
vain thing to look for justification by it.* —MATTHEW HENRY

Adear friend of mine is suffering right now with a painful and debilitating disease. Skilled doctors armed with
state-of-the-art medical diagnostic tests have pinpointed her
problem. They know exactly what is causing her suffering
and have explained it to her in detail. She understands what
they have told her and can discuss her condition intelligently.
However, none of that has alleviated her suffering. Although
she and her doctors know exactly what is wrong, they can
do nothing about it. At the time I am writing, there is no
known cure.

As good, needful, and helpful as state-of-the-art medical diagnostic tests are, they cannot fix anything. They can pinpoint the problem, but they cannot cure it. How foolish my friend would be to keep "going for tests" thinking that undergoing the tests could help her get better. I am grateful that my friend is wiser than that. She herself is a highly trained medical professional, knows the difference between diagnosis and cure, and is not about to waste time, money, and energy on hollow hope.

Unfortunately, the first-century Galatians were not anything like her. When Paul said, "You foolish Galatians," he described them perfectly. They were placing their hope in the law's diagnostic procedures when they *knew* the sure cure was faith in Christ Jesus. Paul had taught them the difference between diagnosis and cure. But the Judaizers had bewitched them with deceptive teaching. The Galatians had been duped by a cleverly crafted lie that may have sounded something like this: *Paul's prescription of hearing with faith is not enough to make you right with God, but do not despair. It can be made fully effective by simply adding a dose of law-keeping.*

Paul challenged that lie because he knew believing it would produce a deadly doctrinal "drug interaction." As a highly trained apostolic professional, he knew that combining law-keeping with faith denatures[1] God's grace—and that denatured grace neither justifies sinners nor equips them for service.

Paul was not saying that the law plays no part in God's plan of salvation. He knew that the law is the perfect spiritual diagnostic device, a sharp "two-edged sword" capable of judging "the thoughts and intentions of the heart." He knew it lays bare the terminal affliction of sin with which we are all infected (Hebrews 4:12–13). He knew it reflects God's holy and righteous character and details His unattainably high standard of absolute perfection for fellowship with Him. He knew it reveals that we all have failed to meet God's requirements and stand convicted and condemned in His holy presence. Paul knew that God's law diagnoses our problem flawlessly. But he also knew that even the best diagnosis cannot cure anything.

Paul knew that curing the sin problem that separates us from God requires having faith in His gracious provision of a sinless Substitute who met God's high standard and paid the wages of sin *on our behalf.* Saving faith trusts in God to do for us what we cannot do for ourselves. Such faith was reckoned as righteousness for Father Abraham and for every redeemed child of God down through the ages.

Interestingly, the law itself testifies of this truth just as clearly as does the gospel. In Galatians 3:10–18, Paul lets God's law speak on behalf of God's grace and concludes from its testimony that the law did not *amend* the gracious promise given to Abraham, but upheld and affirmed it.

## What the Law Says about Grace

### *(Galatians 3:10–14)*

Paul was a preacher of God's gospel of grace but did not view God's law as an opponent. His opponents were those who misused the law because they did not hear and heed God's revelation concerning its purpose. The Old Testament Scriptures, which the Judaizers should have known very well, affirmed that God gave the law as a diagnostic device, not as a cure. God intended His law to be a means of highlighting our need for the gospel of grace, not an addendum to faith or an alternative route to right standing with God.

Paul made his case against his opponents by letting the very law they were touting demolish their argument. His three masterful points are each drawn directly from God's revelation in the Old Testament.

> For as many as are of the works of the Law are under a curse; for it is written, "Cursed is everyone who does not abide by all things written in the book of the law, to perform them." Now that no one is justified by the Law before God is evident; for, "The righteous man shall live by faith." However, the Law is not of faith; on the contrary, "He who practices them shall live by them." (3:10–12)

Paul exalted God's law as a reflection of His holy character, nature, and will. As such, it sets a standard of perfect compliance that no descendant of Adam could ever achieve. Violation of any part of God's law brings the violator under God's curse (Deuteronomy 27:26; James 2:10). Because God is the "Holy One" whose "eyes are too pure to approve evil" and "can not look on wickedness with favor" (Habakkuk 1:12–13), those who break His law are barred from His presence and condemned to spend eternity under His just wrath and punishment (2 Thessalonians 1:6–10).

The law sets God's standard and announces sanctions against transgressors but provides no lasting means of cleansing and forgiveness. The author of Hebrews explained that the law's required sacrifices did not in themselves purge the stain of sin from the lawbreaker. Rather, they pointed the lawbreaker to the coming Redeemer who would keep the law perfectly and pay its penalties on behalf of all whom God had chosen to save (Hebrews 10:1–18). Righteous men and women in the Old Testament were justified (made right with God) by their faith in that coming Redeemer. The prophet Habakkuk said that they "lived" (were freed from sin's curse) by their faith, not by their law-keeping (2:4).

Paul's appeal to Leviticus 18:5 affirmed that faith and law-keeping cannot be combined in an effort to achieve right standing with God. That is because law-keeping relies on personal merit, whereas faith trusts completely in the merit of the Redeemer. Those who approach God on the basis of their own law-keeping will inevitably fall short of His perfect standard, but those who look in faith to the perfect law-keeping[2] of Christ will be made right with God. Fallen sinners are simply unable to *earn* favor with God. God's favor is granted solely by grace.

God's law and His grace are both essential in God's plan of salvation, but each serves a distinct function. Just as diagnostic tests and medical cures contribute uniquely to the same goal of physical health and vitality, God's law and His grace play separate but equally necessary roles in the drama of redemption.

God's law shows us that we are under God's curse and deserve His wrath because of our sin. It also reveals the glory of God's holy character, which His children should reflect in their behavior. God's law condemns sin and sets standards, but it cannot justify sinners or empower them to live lives that glorify God.

God's law pinpoints our problem, highlights our inability to fix it ourselves, and points us to God's gracious provision of a sinless Substitute who did for us what we could not do for ourselves (Acts 13:38–39). It tells us what is wrong, admits it cannot fix it, and directs us to the sure cure of pure grace.

Paul reminded the Galatians that only faith in the work of Christ Jesus and reliance upon the Holy Spirit's enabling power saves and sanctifies sinners.

Christ redeemed us from the curse of the Law, having become a curse for us—for it is written, "Cursed is everyone who hangs on a tree"—in order that in Christ Jesus the blessing of Abraham might come to the Gentiles, so that we would receive the promise of the Spirit through faith. (Galatians 3:13–14)

A few months ago, I attended a conference where one of the plenary speakers tackled the topic of Christian witness through television and movies. Mel Gibson's film *The Passion of the Christ* had recently been released and, to no one's surprise, quickly slid into the spotlight of our discussion.

At one point, the speaker asked us what kinds of comments we were hearing from unsaved folks who had seen the movie. One woman said that the comment she heard most often was this: "How could (or why would) God allow His own Son to be treated so badly?" The speaker responded enthusiastically, "That's a great question! How does it open a door for the gospel?"

After a few moments of silence, somebody said, "Well, it was either Him or us." Frankly, I had never thought of the gospel quite like that. But the longer I think about it, the better I like it. It clearly captures the essence of what theologians call "substitutionary atonement," which lies at the heart of God's gospel of grace.

Paul was referring to substitutionary atonement when he said Christ redeemed us from the curse of the law by becoming a curse for us. Jesus identified with fallen sinners by taking on their humanity (Philippians 2:7–8), living among them, and being tempted in all ways as they are. However, He identified with sinners while remaining sinless Himself (Hebrews 4:15). He obeyed God's law perfectly (Hebrews 5:9) and, therefore, lived as a man without falling under the curse of the law.

Everything He did pleased God the Father (John 8:29), and nothing He did incited God's wrath.

That is why Jesus Christ could stand in our place and atone (make right; pay the price) for our sins. He could become a curse on our behalf because He Himself had not fallen under the curse. If He had violated God's law in any way, the curse that He bore would have been in payment for His sins, not ours.

God's holiness demands that He act justly. His righteousness requires that He punish sin. He would have remained perfectly holy and righteous if He had condemned every sinner to Hell. But aren't we glad that He chose not to do that! We rejoice that God's holiness encompasses love, mercy, and grace as well as justice and wrath. In order to display His own glorious attributes as fully as He desires, God provided a perfect Substitute whose self-sacrificial atonement redeemed us from the curse of the law.

The Greek word translated "redeemed" in this passage is *exagorazō*. It means "buy out of slavery by paying a price."[3] Paul used it to describe Jesus' work of liberating us from the law's curse by paying the penalty our sin incurred. The curse of the law is a divine judgment that sentences lawbreakers to condemnation. God cannot simply suspend our sentence and remain holy and just. His righteousness demands that His wrath be satisfied. The only way He could extend love, mercy, and grace to condemned sinners was to pour out His wrath on a sinless Substitute. And of course, Jesus Christ, the God-man, was the only qualified applicant. It was indeed "Him or us."

God's law demanded that convicted criminals be executed and that their bodies be tied to a post until sunset as a visible sign of their rejection by God (Deuteronomy 21:22–23). Although Jesus never violated God's law, He was crucified—

"hanged on a tree"—because He chose to "become sin" and bear God's curse against every sinner who would be saved through faith in His sacrifice. Jesus' perfect life and atoning death cured the sin problem diagnosed by the law.

Thus, Jesus Christ fulfilled all the requirements of God's holy law and shattered the barrier between Jew and Gentile. Hearing with faith now unites believers of all races, social classes, and gender *in Christ*, grants them the justification promised to Abraham, and gives them God's Holy Spirit as an indwelling presence.

## God's Law Did Not Amend God's Promise

### *(Galatians 3:15–18)*

If you are a fan of murder mysteries (as I am), you are no doubt familiar with scenes like this one: The family patriarch has died, and the family has gathered for the reading of the will. All are soon shocked to discover that, aside from a few token bequests, the family fortune has been bestowed on the family slacker—the one guy who most assuredly did *not* deserve it. The other family members are understandably furious. Each had done much more to earn granddaddy's big bucks than did the slacker. As the presiding attorney explains that the will is "iron-clad" and cannot be broken, furtive glances are exchanged among the spurned heirs. We begin to suspect that the slacker won't live to collect his inheritance.

Two aspects of "last wills and testaments" make them sure harbingers of wrongful death in such stories: (1) at some point their provisions become inviolable; (2) they are based on promises rather than merit. Those two aspects also make them analogous to God's covenant with Abraham. Paul's reference to them helps us understand that God's law given to Moses did not amend His promise given to Abraham.

> Brethren, I speak in terms of human relations: even though it is only a man's covenant, yet when it has been ratified, no one sets it aside or adds conditions to it. Now the promises were spoken to Abraham and to his seed. He does not say, "And to seeds," as referring to many, but rather to one, "And to your seed," that is, Christ. What I am saying is this: the Law, which came four hundred and thirty years later, does not invalidate a covenant previously ratified by God, so as to nullify the promise. For if the inheritance is based on law, it is no longer based on a promise; but God has granted it to Abraham by means of a promise. (3:15–18)

Nearly all legal systems contain provisions for "finalizing" a will. If certain conditions are met, the will cannot be changed thereafter. Paul does not tell us which legal system he had in mind when he spoke of human covenants—probably because it does not matter. His point of analogy is that if human covenants are so characterized, surely God's covenants are too.

God ratified His covenant with Abraham in Genesis 15 as a covenant of promise dependent for fulfillment upon God's faithfulness alone. The promise was made to Abraham and "his seed," or as some translations render it, "his offspring." Both translations are collective nouns, words that can be understood in either a singular or plural sense. However, in this case, Paul does not allow us the option of choosing.

He tells us point blank that God used the term to refer to Jesus Christ. God's promise was made to Abraham and his seed (offspring), Jesus Christ. Abraham was promised justification by faith, and Jesus Christ was promised a people for His own possession who would glorify and enjoy Him forever (John 17:6; Titus 1:14). Those who share Abraham's faith in God's promise and are thereby justified in God's sight make up the people promised to Christ. That group of people, spiritual descendants of Abraham, will, as Paul has emphasized all through Galatians, include both Jews and Gentiles.

The nature of God's promise to Abraham precluded its being amended or invalidated hundreds of years later[4] by God's law given to Moses. God's promise to justify Abraham on account of his faith came with no strings attached. It was a promise, not a contract. It was not conditioned upon Abraham meeting certain requirements. All Abraham had "to do" to receive God's promise was believe God would do what He said He would do. Abraham was justified by hearing with faith, not by keeping the law.

God's law given to Moses did not modify God's promise to Abraham in any way. But that does not mean that God's law has no purpose. In this lesson we have emphasized what the law cannot do. In the next, we will see what it can and must do.

## Notes

1. When something is denatured, its basic properties are changed. Grace is best defined doctrinally as "favor extended against merit." Although most Christians would define grace as "unmerited favor," God actually grants us His *favor* when we have clearly *merited* His wrath. God's grace is, by nature, an astonishing *gift* given to those who deserve punishment. Adding "works of the law" to God's grace changes its basic nature from astonishing gift to

earned reward. Doing so is an exercise in futility since fallen humanity *cannot* merit God's good gift of salvation.

2. Christ's perfect law-keeping included (1) perfect obedience to all God's commandments and (2) bearing the law's sanctions against those lawbreakers God chose to save.

3. James Montgomery Boice, *The Expositor's Bible Commentary*, vol. 10, *Romans–Galatians* (Grand Rapids, Mich.: Zondervan, 1976), 460.

4. Concerns over the accuracy of Paul's dating of the law 430 years after the promise are alleviated simply by counting from God's final reaffirmation of His promise to Jacob rather than from His first affirmation of it to Abraham.

## E X E R C I S E S

### REVIEW

1. Explain how the law functions as a spiritual diagnostic device.

2. How does Paul let the law speak on behalf of God's grace? Explain the three points he makes from the Old Testament to counter the Judaizers' assertion that law-keeping must be added to grace.

3. How does the phrase "It was Him or us" capture the essence of the doctrine of substitutionary atonement? Why is a substitutionary atonement necessary for the salvation of sinners?

4. Explain the significance of Jesus' being "hanged on a tree."

5. What two characteristics of "last wills and testaments" make them analogous to God's covenant with Abraham? How does this analogy help us understand the relationship between God's promise to Abraham and His law given to Moses?

6. Explain the significance of God's promise being made to Abraham and "his seed."

## APPLICATION

1. This week review previous memory verses and begin memorizing one or more of the following Scripture passages:

   2 Corinthians 5:21
   Galatians 3:13
   1 Peter 1:18–19

2. This week in your prayer time, use Romans 3:21–26; Romans 8:1–4; and Ephesians 2:1–10 to help you thank God for your salvation in Christ and seek His power to live out the reality of your union with Him.

3. If you are a Christian, prayerfully consider two truths taught in this lesson: Christ redeemed you from the curse of the law by becoming a curse for you; and you are now united with Him and indwelt by His Holy Spirit. List several practical implications these two truths have on your daily life. (Think, in particular, about how they impact the way you respond to your own sin, the way you pursue your ministry efforts, the way you pray and worship God). If you are not a Christian, ask God in prayer to help you understand what Christ's becoming "a curse for us" means and to give you the faith to believe in Him.

4. List several ways in which the truths you have learned thus far in your study of Galatians have enhanced your effectiveness in fulfilling your chief end of glorifying and enjoying God.

## DIGGING DEEPER

1. Some Bible teachers argue against the doctrine of substitutionary atonement. A few have gone so far as to derisively label it "butchershop theology." Obviously, they find it hard to believe that God would allow His own Son to be treated so badly. Study the following Scripture passages within their contexts, discern what the Bible teaches regarding substitutionary atonement, and then formulate a response to these teachers.

   Exodus 12:13; Leviticus 1:4; 16:20–22; 17:11; Psalm 49:7–8; Isaiah 52:13–53:12; 59:1–21; Matthew 20:28; 26:27–28; Mark 10:45; Luke 22:14–23; John 1:29; 10:11–15; Acts 20:28; Romans 3:24–25; 8:3–4; 1 Corinthians 6:20; 7:23; 2 Corinthians 5:18–21; Galatians 1:4; 2:20; 3:13; Ephesians 1:7; 2:16; Colossians 1:19–23; Hebrews 9:22–28; 1 Peter 1:18–19; 2:24; 3:18; 1 John 1:7; 2:2; 4:10; Revelation 5:9; 7:14.

2. Assume that a close friend of yours is faced with a trial similar to the one I described in the opening paragraphs of this lesson: she has been diagnosed with a painful and debilitating disease for which there is no cure. She has, for many years, been a faithful student of Scripture and understands God's truth fairly well. However, this diagnosis has been understandably difficult for her to accept. As you and she share lunch and discuss her situation, she tells you, "I feel like I am being punished. I do so many things wrong, I guess I should have expected something like this."

   Use what you have learned so far in Galatians to encourage your friend.

*Primary Passage*
GALATIANS 3:19–29

*Supplementary Passages*
EXODUS 19:1–20:17
DEUTERONOMY 5:1–33
ACTS 7:52–53
ROMANS 3:19–31; 4:13–25; 6:8–18; 7:7–12; 8:16–17
1 CORINTHIANS 1:26–31; 15:56–57
2 CORINTHIANS 3:1–11
HEBREWS 2:1–4; 3:1–6
JAMES 2:10
1 JOHN 3:1

Before reading the lesson material, please read the primary
Scripture passage listed above and as many of the supplementary passages as time allows. Then briefly summarize in
your notebook what you have read. (Do not go into detail.
Limit your summary to a brief description of the people,
events, and/or ideas discussed in the passages.)

# The White Light of the Law

*It is only when one submits to the law that one can speak of grace.* —DIETRICH BONHOEFFER

During the past several years, I have spent many hours on airplanes. I have heard flight attendants explain "the safety features of this aircraft" so often, I have the spiel almost memorized. Two sentences in particular are firmly lodged in my mind: "Should evacuation become necessary, track lights in the aisles will be illuminated. White lights lead to red lights and the emergency exits." Perhaps living through one hair-raising scare-in-the-air has heightened my interest in evacuation procedures!

Obviously, illuminated track lighting in the aisles of airplanes cannot "save your life" in the event of an emergency. No matter how well it is working, it will not eliminate or correct the emergency situation, nor will it carry you out of harm's way. But does that mean illuminated track lighting in the aisles of airplanes is of no value in a life-threatening crisis? Of course not! Those little white and red lights in the aisles contribute *significantly* to life saving efforts in at least two ways. They reveal that a life-threatening situation exists; and they point out the way of escape. When endangered passengers believe the testimony of the lights and follow their direction, the chances of survival increase greatly.

Paul tells us in Galatians 3:19–29 that God's law, given to Moses on Sinai, functions in much the same way. Clearly, we can envision humanity's fall into sin as a "crash landing" of sorts. But, we should bear in mind that the very worst airplane disaster pales in comparison to the disaster of sin. When Adam and Eve crashed and burned in the garden of Eden, they took all of humanity with them. Since then folks have struggled to make their way through the twisted wreckage of God's once-perfect creation. At stake is much more than physical life or earthly well-being. Those who stay lost in the rubble will forfeit their souls.

So how, in this world, do we find our way out of sin's devastation? Paul tells us in effect, "The emergency track lighting has been illuminated. The white light of God's law leads to the red light of the gospel and the emergency exit of Jesus Christ."

Paul's words presume that God's law itself cannot save our souls. He has already affirmed that it can neither loosen the grip of sin on our lives nor deflect God's righteous wrath away from us sinners. But he does *not* conclude that the law is therefore useless in our soul-threatening crisis. He heads off another potential objection to the gospel of grace by explaining that God's law contributes *significantly* to soul-saving efforts in at least two ways. It reveals that we are indeed in grave danger of eternal damnation; and it points out the *only* way of escape. When endangered sinners believe its testimony and follow its direction, their "chance" of redemption does much more than increase greatly—it becomes absolutely assured!

## God's Law Reveals That We Are in Grave Danger

### (Galatians 3:19–22)

Like most analogies, my likening God's law to the emergency track lighting on airplanes is not perfect. My analogy's primary flaw is that, although both the law and the lighting reveal grave danger, the impact of that revelation differs greatly. Emergency track lighting on airplanes nearly always confirms danger of which the passengers are acutely aware. However, the law's warning is often denied or resisted by sinners. Folks in a downed aircraft rarely glance at the illuminated white and red lights in the aisle, yawn, and mutter, "Must be some kind of electrical glitch." But those lost in sin who encounter God's law often respond, "Why all the fuss? I'm doing just fine . . . better than most. God knows I do more right than wrong, and He understands nobody's perfect. God isn't angry with me. I'm one of the good guys."

R. C. Sproul says, "The greatest point of unbelief in our culture and in our church today is an unbelief in the wrath of God and in His certain promise of judgment for the human race. . . . People today simply do not believe that there will be a day of judgment. . . . The greatest and most frequent error that human beings make is the assumption that they are going to survive the judgment of a holy God on the basis of their own performance."[1]

The common error Sproul describes yields tragic results.

God's righteousness requires Him to require righteousness of those with whom He has fellowship.[2] His law sets the standard of righteousness required to be admitted into His presence. The standard is *perfection*, which, of course, far exceeds even the best human effort. Because God is holy, He cannot drop the bar to a point we can clear. The only score He can accept is 100 percent. His holiness means He cannot grade on a curve.

Many people today do not understand that. They look at God's law as instruction in self-righteousness that earns favor with God. But that is not the purpose for which God's law was given. Paul told the Galatians that God's law was given to demolish all thoughts of self-righteous merit and leave sinners with no hope of being made right with Him by their own efforts.

> Why the Law then? It was added because of transgressions, having been ordained through angels by the agency of a mediator, until the seed would come to whom the promise had been made. Now a mediator is not for one party only; whereas God is only one. Is the Law then contrary to the promises of God? May it never be! For if a law had been given which was able to impart life, then righteousness would indeed have been based on law. But the Scripture has shut up everyone under sin, so that the promise by faith in Jesus Christ might be given to those who believe. (3:19–22)

A few years ago, I read an intriguing book in which the author emphasized that most "evangelism methods" start at the wrong place—with the gracious salvation provided by Jesus Christ. He said that was the wrong starting place because sinners cannot understand grace until they understand sin, and they cannot understand sin until they understand the holiness of God. The author advocated an evangelism method that *first* explains God's holy and righteous character, *then* describes the unbreachable chasm sin created between God and fallen humanity, and *finally*, announces that God has established a means of breaching the chasm in the gracious gift of His Son.[3]

The author supported his views by explaining that the Bible itself takes this approach to evangelism. The Bible presents the gospel of grace within an extensive, well-developed *context* detailing the tension between God's holiness and humanity's sin. Although God's promise of salvation is first revealed in the early chapters of Genesis and faithfully reiterated throughout the Old Testament, it is only fully explained in the apostolic epistles. The majority of the Bible is context for the gospel—essential context without which the gospel cannot be rightly understood or applied.

God's law is part of that essential context. Paul says that it was "added" to the promise "because of transgressions." Commentators disagree on the precise meaning of this phrase; however, the discussions affirm one basic idea. God's law *defined* sin as transgression against God. The word translated "transgression" (*parabasis*) means to step beyond or to cross a fixed boundary into forbidden territory.[4] God's holy nature is reflected in His standards for human conduct. Thus, disobedience to His law is a transgression against *Him*. It is an affront to His righteousness and incites His wrath.

Since every son of Adam and daughter of Eve is a sinner by nature, the "white light" of God's law announces that we are all in grave danger. Since all of God's law is infused with His holiness, any slight violation makes us "guilty of all" (James 2:10). It is foolish to look at the law as instruction in self-righteousness that earns favor with God. No fallen human has ever been able to meet its demands.

God's law does not allow us to judge our performance in comparison to other people. It requires of all people perfect obedience to all its commands. God's law does not affirm how well we are doing. Instead, it acts much as would a prosecuting attorney, judge, and jury when handed an airtight case against the defendant. It proves our transgressions, declares us undeniably "guilty," and sentences us to eternal separation from God. Tim Keller captured the essence of the way the law works when he said, "Ironically, if we think we can be righteous by the law, we have missed the point of the law."[5]

Paul emphasizes the distinction between God's law and His promise while underscoring that the two do not contradict one another. The fact that the law was given by the agency of a mediator (most likely a reference to Moses) indicates that it is by nature a contract between God and His people. God laid down requirements, which His people agreed to perform (Exodus 19:1–9). On the other hand, the promise given to Abraham and his seed (whom Paul has already identified as Jesus Christ) is by nature a will or a testament. God bestows the no-strings-attached gift of being part of a people for Christ's own possession on chosen sinners who deserve only wrath.

The law and the promise work in harmony because they are not alternative means of being made right with God. The law cannot do what the promise does—impart life to fallen sinners. But it can and does alert fallen sinners to their desperate condition and point them toward the only means of escape.

## God's Law Points Out the Only Way of Escape

### *(Galatians 3:23–29)*

The emergency track lighting in the aisles of airplanes would be tragically useless to imperiled passengers if it consisted solely of white lights leading nowhere. If all it did were confirm the grave danger of the passengers' situation without pointing out the way of escape, it would not help them at all. In much the same way, if God had given us nothing more than His law, we would have no hope of ever being made right with Him.

Fortunately, the emergency track lighting system does not work that way. And by God's glorious grace, His law does not work that way either. Just as white lights lead to red lights and the emergency exits, God's law points to His gospel and His Son Jesus Christ. Paul likens God's law to a custodian or a guardian whose restrictive rule over us highlights our inability to help ourselves and directs us to the Savior and Lord who alone can deliver us.

> But before faith came, we were kept in custody under the law, being shut up to the faith which was later to be revealed. Therefore the Law has become our tutor to lead us to Christ, so that we may be justified by faith. But now that faith has come, we are no longer under a tutor. (3:23–25)

Before we came to faith in Jesus Christ, Paul explains, the law functioned as a "tutor" who "kept us in custody."[6] The Greek word translated "tutor" is *paidagōgos*. It was used in Paul's day in reference to a slave charged with the duties of minding, directing, disciplining, and guarding young boys until they grew up and were able to care for themselves.

Tutors were typically very strict, confining the boy's natural bent toward disobedience within the bounds of rigorous discipline. Although the young boys may not always have agreed, the tutors (and the fathers who put them in charge) knew such constraint was in the boys' best interests. The tutors' restrictive discipline taught the boys to exercise the self-control needed to fulfill the responsibilities of adulthood.

In much the same way, God's law confines those without faith in Christ within its strict control. It lays down the rules and imposes penalties for disobedience. It defines sin as transgression against our holy and righteous God and condemns our inability to live up to its standards. It teaches us about God's righteous requirements and makes us fear judgment. The law convicts us of sin, but does not forgive us. It coerces compliance, but does not change hearts. It demands perfection, but does not make us perfect.[7]

If the law did not point us to Christ as the means of forgiveness, heart-change, and imputed perfection, it would give us no hope and shut us up to despair. Just as the rule of a *paidagōgos* was meant to prepare Greek boys for manhood, God's law was meant to prepare God's chosen children for the coming of faith.

Faith in Christ Jesus makes us "sons of God."[8] When we exercise God-given faith in what Christ has done for us, we are justified before God and enter into a new relationship with Him. We become His adopted children "in Christ," true descendants of Abraham and fellow heirs of the promise.

> For you are all sons of God through faith in Christ Jesus. For all of you who were baptized into Christ have clothed yourselves with Christ. There is neither Jew nor Greek, there is neither slave nor free man, there is neither male nor female; for you are all one in Christ Jesus. And if you belong to Christ, then you are Abraham's descendants, heirs according to promise. (3:26–29)

Paul may have been reminding the Galatians that they *already had* in their union with Christ what the Judaizers were trying to give them through law-keeping. Jesus Christ had kept the law perfectly on their behalf and fully satisfied God's wrath against their transgressions (Romans 8:3–4; 1 Peter 2:24). Their faith in His work secured their adoption into God's family.

As "sons of God," they now enjoyed a permanent, loving Father-child relationship with Him (John 10:27–29), the right of immediate access to His presence (Romans 5:1–2), confident expectation of blessing from Him (Luke 11:11–13; Romans 8:32), security in His provision of their every need (Matthew 6:31–34), the promise of greater things to come (Romans 8:16–17; 1 John 3:2), and a share in the eternal inheritance of Jesus Christ (Luke 12:32; 1 Peter 1:3–5).[9] The law cannot provide any of these things. It can only point to the One who can.

Because sons of God are united with Christ, they are also one with each other. Distinctions between us remain, but no longer divide. The sins of pride, greed, and lust that build walls between races, classes, and genders can only be fully conquered in Christ by the power of His Holy Spirit. And that divine unity transcends our present-day and local churches. We are one with all those throughout history and into eternity who share Abraham's faith.

Edgar Andrews expresses my joy as I contemplate the unity I share with my brothers and sisters of all races and classes throughout the ages: "Here is food and drink for the soul. Here is the ground of love for God. Here is a reason for heartfelt worship. Here lies our confidence in prayer. Here is hope in darkness and joy in adversity. Here is the burial-ground of fears. Here rise the springs of courage, boldness, and active service!"[10] Praise be to God for His indescribable gift!

## Notes

1. R. C. Sproul, *Saved from What?* (Wheaton, Ill.: Crossway, 2002), 23, 32.

2. I borrowed this phrase from Thomas Chalmers, who defined the righteousness of God as that righteousness which His righteousness requires Him to require. Unfortunately, I have lost the specific reference.

3. Although this fine author's excellent point about evangelism has stuck in my mind, his name and the title of his book have not. This is unfortunate as I would love to give credit for work well done.

4. Kenneth S. Wuest, *Wuest's Word Studies from the Greek New Testament for the English Reader*, vol. 1, *Mark, Romans, Galatians, Ephesians and Colossians* (Grand Rapids, Mich.: Eerdmans), 104.

5. Tim Keller, *Paul's Letter to the Galatians: Living in Line with the Truth of the Gospel, Leaders' Guide* (New York: Redeemer Presbyterian Church, 2002). Leader's notes for question #4, lesson 6: "The Gospel and the Law." Downloaded from Redeemer Presbyterian Church Web site (www.redeemer.com). No page numbers.

6. Paul's illustration is understood in two ways by most commentators: either as describing the historical role played by the law in the nation of Israel, or as the typical role played by the law in the lives of those chosen for salvation. I am taking it in the second sense primarily because most of the Galatians who originally read Paul's letter were Gentiles. They had no "history" with God's law, but they could certainly understand it as a convicting and directing device.

7. This is not to say that the law's inabilities make it imperfect. The law does perfectly what God designed it to do.

8. The word "son" used in this context refers to "heirs" rather than male offspring. It includes women as well as men.

9. Most of this list came from Edgar H. Andrews, *Free in Christ: The Message of Galatians*, The Welwyn Commentary Series (Durham, England: Evangelical Press, 1996), 188.
10. Ibid.

## E x e r c i s e s

### Review

1. In what two ways does God's law contribute significantly to soul-saving efforts?
2. Explain how God's law reveals the danger sinners are in.
3. What does the word "transgression" (*parabasis*) mean? How does understanding the meaning of this word help you understand the role of God's law in His plan of salvation?
4. Distinguish between the nature of God's law and His promise. Then explain why they do not contradict one another.
5. Explain the role of a "tutor" (*paidagōgos*) in the life of Greek boys. How does God's law function similarly in the lives of those God chooses for salvation?
6. List some of the benefits associated with being a "son of God." (Feel free to add to those listed in the lesson, including scriptural support.)
7. How does being united with Christ affect our relationship with other Christians?

### Application

1. This week review previous memory verses and begin memorizing one or more of the following Scripture passages:

   Romans 6:14–15

1 Corinthians 15:56–57
James 2:10

2. This week in your prayer time, use Romans 6:1–23 to deepen your appreciation for your freedom in Christ and to thank God for your "liberation" from sin's dominion.

3. Develop a brief outline which will help you share God's gospel of grace according to the method suggested on pages 96–97. Include "summary" statements of each major point in your outline, along with supporting Scripture passages. Work with a friend if you prefer, and feel free to seek help from your pastor or another leader or teacher in your church. Review your outline and practice it with another Christian. Then pray for one or more opportunities this week to use your outline in a "real-life" situation—and for the courage to speak when those opportunities arise.

4. Before the coming of Christ, Jewish men were taught to pray: "Blessed art Thou, O Lord our God, King of the Universe, who hast not made me a foreigner; Blessed art Thou, O Lord our God, King of the Universe, who hast not made me a slave; Blessed art Thou, O Lord our God, King of the Universe, who hast not made me a woman." And Jewish women were taught to pray, "Blessed art Thou, O Lord our God, King of the Universe, who hast made me according to your will." Using what you have learned from Paul in this lesson, rewrite these prayers, combining them into one prayer that all "sons of God through faith in Christ" should be delighted to pray. (Recall that the term "sons" in this context has to do with inheritance rather than gender.)

## DIGGING DEEPER

In his book *The God Who Justifies*, James R. White said, "*Every fundamental error regarding the doctrine of justification that man has ever invented flows from a denial of the nature and impact of sin in man's life.* Indeed when one allows man to make *any* kind of response to God, to cling to *any* shred of self-righteousness, the result will *always* be an addition to faith alone as the means of justification. Justification becomes a process, a cooperative effort, as soon as the defendant is allowed to make excuses for himself. The *sola* in the great Reformation credo *sola fide* ("faith alone")—faith without the addition of any meritorious human actions—dies the death of a thousand qualifications whenever man's deadness in sin is compromised" (James R. White, *The God Who Justifies* [Minneapolis: Bethany, 2001], 51, emphasis in the original). Based on what you have learned thus far in Galatians, do you think White's comments are consistent with what Paul teaches in Galatians and Romans? Support your answer with specific references.

### Primary Passage
GALATIANS 4:1–11

### Supplementary Passages
DEUTERONOMY 7:6–8; 10:14–17
1 SAMUEL 16:6–7
PSALM 16:5–11
MARK 14:35–36
JOHN 10:27–30; 14:6–11; 15:16; 17:3
ACTS 14:8–18
ROMANS 8:1–17; 14:5–9
1 CORINTHIANS 2:9–10
2 CORINTHIANS 4:6; 8:9
EPHESIANS 1:1–14; 2:1–22
COLOSSIANS 2:6–8, 16–23
1 THESSALONIANS 1:8–12
2 TIMOTHY 1:8–14; 2:19
TITUS 1:1–3
HEBREWS 2:14–18; 4:14–16
1 JOHN 2:24–25; 3:7–15; 5:10–13

Before reading the lesson material, please read the primary Scripture passage listed above and as many of the supplementary passages as time allows. Then briefly summarize in your notebook what you have read. (Do not go into detail. Limit your summary to a brief description of the people, events, and/or ideas discussed in the passages.)

# Heirs, Slaves, and Sons

*People who prefer the law to the gospel are like Aesop's dog*
*who let go of the meat to snatch at the shadow in the water.*
—Martin Luther

Remember Cinderella? Through a series of fairy-tale circumstances, the poor girl ended up losing mother and father to death and being forced to live in bondage to a wicked stepmother and two ugly stepsisters. Then through another series of fairy-tale circumstances, she broke free of her bondage by marrying the handsome and loving prince of the realm. As expected, the fairy tale ends by declaring, "They lived happily ever after."

But what if the story had ended this way: "Cinderella and her new princely husband moved to another realm and lived miserably ever after under the thumb of a wicked monarch and two ugly henchmen." Ridiculous, you say? Absolutely, I say. But no more ridiculous than what the Galatians were doing. Disdaining the freedom of salvation in Christ, they were embracing a bondage just like the one they had already escaped.

In Galatians 4:1–11, Paul emphasizes just how foolish that was. With well-disciplined patience struggling to control irritated discouragement, he urged his bumbling, bewitched brethren to appreciate and rejoice in what they had become so they would not return to what they had been.

## Elemental, My Dear Galatians

### *(Galatians 4:1–3)*

By the time Paul arrived at this point in his letter, he had effectively argued that redeemed Jews and Gentiles are *one* in Christ Jesus. He had conclusively demonstrated that *all* sinners who exercise God-given faith to believe and trust in the work of God's Son are clothed in His righteousness and adopted into God's family. He had firmly established that the coming of Christ demolished the dividing wall between Jew and Gentile by offering salvation to all sinners solely on the basis of repentance and faith.

Paul had explained that the law given to Moses was never intended as a means of salvation. Rather, its purpose was to make sinners aware of their desperate state and drive them to Christ as their only hope of escaping God's wrath. He had made clear that Jew and Gentile alike who looked to Christ for salvation were united in Him as true descendants of Abraham, "heirs according to promise."

And now he affirms that all *heirs de facto* (heirs in fact) were once *heirs de jure* (heirs by right), whose paths to salvation may have looked very different but were really quite similar.

> Now I say, as long as the heir is a child, he does not differ at all from a slave although he is owner of everything, but he is under guardians and managers until the date set by the father. So also we, while we were children, were held in bondage under the elemental things of the world. (4:1–3)

Paul alluded to worldly inheritance rites to remind the Galatians that all those who belong to Christ (Jew and Gentile alike) were designated as "heirs according to promise" long before they were saved. *All* true "descendants of Abraham" were chosen in Christ and predestined to adoption as sons "before the foundation of the world" (Ephesians 1:4–5). God promised them to His Son as a people for His own possession "before the ages began" (Titus 1:1–3; 2:13–14 ESV). Some "heirs according to promise" came to faith in the nation of Israel by looking forward to and trusting in what God's promised Redeemer *would* do. Many more have come to faith by looking back and trusting in what that Redeemer *did* do.

All were "heirs by right" the moment God chose them; but none became "heirs in fact" until they believed in the work of Christ Jesus. From the time of their birth until they believed, Paul likens them to worldly heirs who have not yet arrived at "the date set by the father" and are still under the rule of "guardians and managers."[1] They are no different from slaves, he says, although they are "owners of everything."

In Paul's day "heirs by right" who were not yet "heirs in fact" came in two basic varieties—Jew and Gentile. The Jewish variety lived under the rule of the law; whereas the Gentile variety lived under the rule of various pagan religions. Their lives looked quite different to the outside observer, but Paul tells us they shared one significant characteristic: All were "held in bondage under the elemental things of the world."

The Greek word translated "elemental things" is *stoicheion*, which is used to describe foundational or rudimentary orderliness. (It refers, for example, to the letters of the alphabet.) Paul, however, did not clarify precisely what he had in mind when he used the term. Bible scholars characteristically differ in their attempts to read his mind, so it is difficult to be sure about what he meant. I tend to agree with those commentators who suggest that, given the context, Paul is most likely referring to basic, elemental aspects of *human* religions that promote and rely on works-righteousness instead of faith in Christ Jesus.

William Hendriksen describes elemental things as religious teachings emphasizing rules and regulations by which "people, both Jews and Gentiles, each in their own way, attempted by their own efforts and in accordance with the promptings of their own fleshly (unregenerate) nature, to achieve salvation."[2] John MacArthur says, "The elemental things of all human religion, whether Jewish or Gentile, ancient or modern, inevitably involve the idea of achieving divine acceptance by one's own efforts."[3] And Edgar Andrews adds, "It is belief in the *efficacy* of law-keeping, or of works generally, to justify or purify the sinner, that constitutes a basic tenet of the world and brings human beings into bondage."[4]

I believe this view is consistent with what Paul has already said in this letter and with what he teaches in his other letters. It supports his emphasis on salvation by faith rather than works, strengthens his appeal to Jews and Gentiles to come to Christ in exactly the same way, and sustains his high view of God's law as innately superior to pagan practices.

Given the immediate context of Galatians and the broader context of his other letters, I do *not* believe Paul is grouping God's law together with pagan religions and labeling the lot of them "elemental principles of the world." Rather, he seems to be addressing the *mind-set* of unredeemed Jews and Gentiles who look to human works as the means of being made right with their God (or gods.) He seems to be describing the tendency of Jews and Gentiles alike to think that their deity (true or false) can be appeased and satisfied by acts of human worship, devotion, or sacrifice.

Rather than categorizing God's law with pagan religions, Paul appears to be bundling the false doctrines of legalistic Jews together with the idolatrous practices of pagan Gentiles. He appears to be emphasizing that Jewish unbelievers who trust in their law-keeping are really no different from Gentile unbelievers who trust in their pagan rituals. Both are "held in bondage" under futile, deceptive, religious beliefs.

However, those chosen by God for salvation in both groups are heirs-by-right although not yet heirs-in-fact. They are "children" who are, as yet, no different from slaves. As such they are temporarily bound by the elemental principles of the world, but ultimately destined to receive the full rights, privileges, and responsibilities of sons on the date set by the father.

## You Are Now Sons!

### *(Galatians 4:4–7)*

A television talk-show host once asked a virile, muscular, good-looking film star, "When does a boy become a man?" His unexpected response caught most of the audience completely off guard. "A boy becomes a man," he said. "When his daddy says he's a man."

The ensuing few moments of uncomfortable silence broken by a smattering of nervous laughter validated the truth of what he had said. The audience reaction reflected that even in our individualistic, independence-minded culture, the manliest of men don't think themselves so as long as their daddies are calling them "boys."

Ancient cultures may well have dealt with this phenomenon better than we do. Many of them held formal ceremonies in which boys (and sometimes girls) were officially acknowledged by their fathers (and consequently by the community) to be adults. Paul may have had the Roman ceremony, called the Liberalia, in mind when he wrote this passage. On the seventeenth of March each year, a Roman father could exercise his prerogative to acknowledge his child as an adult by formally adopting him as his acknowledged son and heir at this sacred family festival.[5]

In much the same way, Paul explains, God set a date in eternity past on which He would officially acknowledge those He had chosen as sons and heirs.

> But when the fullness of the time came, God sent forth His Son, born of a woman, born under the Law, so that He might redeem those who were under the Law, that we might receive the adoption as sons. Because you are sons, God has sent forth the Spirit of His Son into our hearts, crying, "Abba! Father!" Therefore you are no longer a slave, but a son; and if a son, then an heir through God." (4:4–7)

God's "Liberalia" was the incarnation of Jesus Christ. When the "fullness of the time came"—when all preparations were complete, the stage was set, and the world was ready—God placed

His Son in the womb of a Jewish woman and caused Him to be born in the likeness of sinful humanity. The baby Mary bore in a stable in Bethlehem was fully God and fully man—fully sinless and pure while fully identified with fallen sinners. He was "born under the Law"—subject to all of its obligations and sanctions. As He grew, lived, and died as a man, He fulfilled the law perfectly, keeping every commandment and bearing the prescribed penalty for every infraction committed by those whom God had chosen as sons and heirs.

Jesus obeyed the law and absorbed its curse so that God's *heirs de jure* could become *heirs de facto*. Jesus did for them what they could not do for themselves with all their legalistic and pagan practices. As their Substitute, He gave them credit for His righteous life and absorbed all of God's wrath against their sin. When God raised Christ from the dead, He proclaimed His satisfaction with the work of His Son, guaranteeing His chosen children "the adoption as sons."[6]

God redeems us for the purpose of adopting us as His children. Salvation is more than a rescue from hell. It is a warm welcome into God's house. God embraces us as His own by uniting us with His Son through the gift of the indwelling Spirit. The Spirit bears witness to the reality of our adoption by crying "Abba! Father!" from His residence within our hearts. His presence equips us to bear fruit for God's glory, to appropriate His truth, and approach Him in prayer. God's Spirit within us seals us as His own and guarantees our inheritance.

Scot McKnight says, as "sons of God," we no longer bear the guilt of our sin before God, fear His wrath, or tremble under the curse of His law. Instead, we are forgiven and freed from condemnation, welcomed into God's family, and led by His Spirit.[7] For believers in Christ, the day appointed by the Father has come.[8] We have been adopted as sons and heirs. We are *no longer* "no different from slaves." How foolish we would be to trade what we are now for what we once were! And yet, Paul said, that was precisely what the Galatians were doing.

## Don't Return to Slavery!

### *(Galatians 4:8–11)*

Although Paul was clearly irritated with the Galatians and may well have been struggling with encroaching discouragement, he loved them far too much to throw in the towel. Rather than write them off as hopelessly senseless and not worth his effort, he diligently pursued them with pointed persuasion.

> However at that time, when you did not know God, you were slaves to those which by nature are no gods. But now that you have come to know God, or rather to be known by God, how is it that you turn back again to the weak and worthless elemental things, to which you desire to be enslaved all over again? You observe days and months and seasons and years. I fear for you, that perhaps I have labored over you in vain. (4:8–11)

Paul appealed to these folks, not as those who were openly rebellious, but as those who were genuinely deceived. He approached them, not as those deliberately opposing him, but as those honestly ignorant of their own foolishness. He had no intention of beating them up, but every intention of exposing their folly. He addressed them, not in fed-up anger, but with pastoral concern.

First, he reminded them of what they had been—worshippers of false gods, enslaved to idols. They had come to know the true God who had known them before time began. When they were in pagan bondage, they had been God's heirs-by-right,

destined to become heirs-in-fact. On the day set by God and by
His grace alone, they had been adopted into God's family, united
with Christ, and filled with His Spirit. They had been freed to live
righteously in the power of His Spirit for the purpose of reflecting
His glory. They were in full possession of all the rights, privileges,
and responsibilities of true sons of God—and yet appeared to be
desiring slavery all over again!

The false doctrine of legalistic Judaizers, Paul told them, was
just as weak and worthless as the barren paganism from which they
had been freed. Neither had any power to save; neither provided
any eternal benefit. Both were worldly "elemental things" offering
nothing but slavery.

Paul confronted them with hard evidence of their foolish
bewitchment. They were legalistically observing Jewish rituals
(days, months, seasons, and years), looking to them as a means of
gaining favor with God. They had taken step one toward return-
ing to bondage. And Paul wrote to prevent them from taking
step two.

"I fear for you," he cried. "Perhaps I have labored over you
in vain." Did they indeed understand and receive the gospel he
preached to them? If so, they would have to turn away from the
empty and impotent elemental things of the world and live in the
blessed freedom of redeemed sons and heirs.

### Notes

1. Most commentators agree that there is very little difference
   between the Greek terms translated "guardians" and "managers." They refer to those slaves who had almost full charge
   over the child-heir until he was grown. Ronald Fung suggests that both terms most likely refer to the same general

office—that of trustees of estates (Ronald Y. K. Fung, *The Epistle to the Galatians* [Grand Rapids, Mich.: Eerdmans], 180). And F. F. Bruce says that if the terms are to be distinguished, the "guardian" would look after the child and the "manager" would look after the child's property (F. F. Bruce, *The Epistle to the Galatians,* The New International Greek Testament Commentary [Grand Rapids, Mich.: Paternoster Press; Eerdmans, 1982], 192). Both are more general terms than the word used in Galatians 3:24 to refer to the law as a "tutor."

2. William Hendriksen, *New Testament Commentary: Galatians, Ephesians, Philippians, Colossians, and Philemon* (Grand Rapids, Mich.: Baker, 1996), 157.

3. John MacArthur Jr., *Galatians*, The MacArthur New Testament Commentary (Chicago: Moody Press, 1987), 105.

4. Edgar H. Andrews, *Free in Christ: The Message of Galatians*, The Welwyn Commentary Series (Durham, England: Evangelical Press, 1996), 202.

5. James Montgomery Boice, *The Expositor's Bible Commentary*, vol. 10, *Romans–Galatians* (Grand Rapids, Mich.: Zondervan, 1976), 471.

6. Recall from the previous lesson that the term "son" in this context has to do with inheritance rather than gender.

7. Scot McKnight, *Galatians*, The NIV Application Commentary (Grand Rapids, Mich.: Zondervan, 1995), 213.

8. For old-covenant believing Jews who looked forward in faith to the work of Christ, "the day set by the Father" was the coming of Christ. For new-covenant believers in Christ, "the day set by the Father" is the day God's Holy Spirit regenerates them and gives them the faith to believe in what Christ has done for them.

## E X E R C I S E S

### REVIEW

1. Distinguish between *heirs de facto* and *heirs de jure*. How do these terms apply to the first-century Christians to whom Paul wrote the book of Galatians?

2. Explain, in your own words, what commentators William Hendriksen, John MacArthur, and Edgar Andrews believe Paul meant when he used the term "elemental principles of the world." According to their view, how are "heirs by right" who are not yet "heirs in fact" (Jews and pagans alike) "no different than slaves"?

3. What was God's "Liberalia"? What is the significance of this event for God's heirs by right?

4. What happens to "heirs by right" who are not yet "heirs in fact" when they are adopted as sons and heirs of God? Can you give personal testimony of this happening in your own life? If so, write out your personal testimony and use it as the basis for a prayer of thanksgiving to God.

5. Describe Paul's appeal to the Galatians *not* to return to what they had been. What do you find most persuasive about it?

### APPLICATION

1. This week review previous memory verses and begin memorizing one or more of the following Scripture passages:

John 15:16

2 Corinthians 8:9

Hebrews 2:17–18

2. This week in your prayer time, use Ephesians 1:1–14 and Titus 1:1–3 to help you praise God for His eternal plan of redemption and to thank Him for choosing you for salvation before time began.

3. If you are a believer in Jesus Christ who can remember the time of your conversion, describe how you were held in bondage by the elemental things of the world before your salvation. Then describe how you have changed since placing your faith in Jesus Christ. Are you ever tempted to return to the weak and worthless elemental things that once enslaved you? How does God pursue and persuade you to return to Him when you are so tempted?

4. Ponder what God says in His Word about you as His "son and heir." Begin with John 17:1–26; Romans 8:1, 31–39; 1 Corinthians 2:6–16; Ephesians 1:1–14; Titus 1:1–3; 1 Peter 1:3–12; and 2 Peter 1:1–4. Use a concordance and consult with other believers to find more verses that describe who you are as God's son and heir. Then write a description of yourself based on the truths found in these verses. Are your thoughts, attitudes, and actions typically consistent with who the Bible says you are as a believer? If not, what specific changes do you need to make to begin living more consistently with who the Bible says you are as a believer? How is living this way different from legalistically adhering to rules and regulations as a means of gaining God's approval?

DIGGING DEEPER

Investigate what a few other commentators believe Paul meant when he used the term "elemental principles of the world." Does their understanding of this term differ from that of Hendriksen, MacArthur, and Andrews? Read Galatians again carefully along with several of Paul's other letters. Based on the immediate context of the book of Galatians and the broader context of Paul's other letters, what do you think he meant when he used this phrase? Discuss your research and conclusions with your pastor and/or elders to gain additional insight into this passage of Scripture.

***Primary Passage***
GALATIANS 4:12–20

***Supplementary Passages***
MATTHEW 10:40–42; 23:1–15
LUKE 10:13–16
JOHN 13:12–20
ROMANS 8:28–39
1 CORINTHIANS 4:14–21; 9:19–27; 10:31–11:1
2 CORINTHIANS 3:18; 12:7–10
EPHESIANS 4:14–24
PHILIPPIANS 3:1–21
COLOSSIANS 1:24–2:5; 3:9–11
1 THESSALONIANS 2:5–20
2 TIMOTHY 3:10–17
1 PETER 5:1–11

Before reading the lesson material, please read the primary
Scripture passage listed above and as many of the supplementary passages as time allows. Then briefly summarize in
your notebook what you have read. (Do not go into detail.
Limit your summary to a brief description of the people,
events, and/or ideas discussed in the passages.)

# "The Perfect Pastor"

*If ministers wish to do any good, let them labor to*
*form Christ, not to form themselves in their hearers.*
—JOHN CALVIN

———— ✦ ————

I recently came across this tongue-in-cheek portrait of "The Perfect Pastor."

He preaches exactly twenty minutes and then sits down. He condemns sin, but never hurts anyone's feelings. He works from 8 AM to 10 PM in every type of work from preaching to custodial

service. He gives . . . [generously] to the church. He also stands
ready to contribute to every good work that comes along. He
is twenty-six years old and has been preaching for thirty years.
He is tall and short, thin, heavyset, and handsome. He has one
brown eye and one blue, hair parted down the middle, left side
dark and straight, the right, brown and wavy. He has a burning desire to work with teenagers and spends all his time with
older folks. He smiles all the time with a straight face because
he has a sense of humor that keeps him seriously dedicated to
his work. He makes fifteen calls a day on church members,
spends all his time evangelizing the unchurched, and is never
out of his office.[1]

I imagine you smiled as you read that facetious sketch, just
as I did. And I hope you were also a little uncomfortable—just
as I was. The humor in that picture is convicting, isn't it? It's
convicting because it exaggerates to the point of absurdity the
foolishness with most congregations evaluate pastors. Sadly,
most of us tend to be more concerned with our pastor's appearance, mannerisms, speaking ability, availability, and demeanor
than we are with his faithfulness to God's Word and concern
for our spiritual welfare. Even more sadly, some pastors cater
to the foolishness of their congregations in order to build up
large followings and enhance their prestige in the Christian
community.

This sad tendency of both people and pastors is no new phenomenon. Paul felt the sting of unworthy criticism and grieved
over the fickleness of congregations led astray by self-serving
pseudo-shepherds. The Galatians, in particular, fell under the
spell of smooth-talking Judaizers who denigrated Paul's apostolic authority and opposed the gospel he preached. Those false
teachers enticed the Galatians with lavish attention laced with

false doctrine. Their intent was to turn the Galatians away from their deep devotion to Paul who, although admittedly not a perfect pastor, came pretty close.

You know as well as I do that "the perfect pastor" is not the one described a few paragraphs earlier. Rather, he is one who faithfully teaches and models the infallible truths revealed in God's Word for the purpose of conforming those under his care to the image of Christ. He loves people enough to make their spiritual welfare his highest priority. And that love compels him to willingly endure all things for the sake of the chosen.

Paul came as close to being a "perfect pastor" as anyone I know of. He taught his congregations well. And when his Galatian sheep went stray, he went after them—not for his own sake, but for theirs. Timothy George explains that Paul was "not interested in developing a personality cult, a band of Pauline groupies, whose primary loyalty would be to him rather than to the gospel."[2] Paul was not miffed because the Galatians were attracted by other teachers; he was distressed because they were entranced by doctrinal spin doctors. He pursued them, not to restore his own numbers, but to renew their commitment to the true gospel of grace.

In Galatians 4:12–20, we see Paul's deep love for his readers clearly revealed. His words in these verses wrap a velvet glove of warm personal appeal around the iron hand of firm exhortation. They break the tension of necessary correction by appealing to the Galatians on the basis of their initial affection for him and his own selfless desire to see Christ formed in them.

## Remember Your Love?

### *(Galatians 4:12–15)*

To this point in his letter, Paul has soundly admonished the Galatians with self-defense and hard-hitting theology. He has figuratively jerked them out of the path of an oncoming truck labeled "legalism" by clearly asserting his apostolic authority and boldly affirming the true gospel of grace. He reminds us of a good parent rushing to rescue a beloved child whose own foolishness has put her in danger. The good parental first response in such cases is to act decisively, authoritatively, and correctively.

But—after such action is taken, most good parents cannot resist enfolding their beloved foolish children in a warm embrace. Good pastors behave a lot like good parents. Paul certainly did. Having asserted his apostolic authority and used it decisively to invalidate the false doctrines of Judaizers, he now seems compelled to wrap his readers in a verbal hug.

> I beg of you, brethren, become as I am, for I also have become as you are. You have done me no wrong; but you know that it was because of a bodily illness that I preached the gospel to you the first time; and that which was a trial to you in my bodily condition you did not despise or loathe, but you received me as an angel of God, as Christ Jesus Himself. Where then is that sense of blessing you had? For I bear you witness that, if possible, you would have plucked out your eyes and given them to me. (4:12–15)

Good pastoring, just like good parenting, is a balancing act. It requires exercising legitimate, necessary authority within the context of clearly evident love and concern. Good pastors, just like good parents, know that their congregations will be most secure, content, and effective when gently led by the firm hand of a pastor who loves them deeply and has their best interests at heart.

Paul's intense defense and correction in the first half of Galatians culminates in an expression of deep concern that he might have labored over them in vain (4:11). However, the very next verse reveals that he was not primarily concerned about wasting his time. No! Paul was distressed by the frightening possibility that, in the final analysis, the Galatians might not share what he had in Christ. He loved them so much that he recoiled at the very idea that they might turn back to the elemental things that once held them in bondage.

Notice that Galatians 4:12 does not contain a complaint that he had wasted his time preaching to them. It contains a plea to "become as I am, for I also have become as you are." Paul had been held in bondage by the elemental things of the world just as they had. His commitment to legalism had imprisoned him under the law just as ruthlessly as had their commitment to pagan religious practices.[3] But he had been freed from that bondage by faith in Christ. And now his deepest desire for the Galatians was that they would know the same freedom he knew—which could only be found in God's gospel of grace.

Paul was not holding a grudge or cherishing personal offense because of the Galatians' foolish behavior. "You have done me no wrong," he assured them, implying that their behavior was not a rejection of him so much as it was a rejection of true freedom in Christ. His strong reaction to their defection was most likely motivated by deep concern for their ultimate welfare, not his own hurt feelings.[4]

He went on to remind them that their earlier fondness for him had resulted from their faithful response to his message, not from their attraction to his appearance, mannerisms, speaking ability, attentiveness, availability, or demeanor. In fact, when he first visited them, the only attractive thing about him was his message! He was ill, suffering repulsive symptoms that would have deterred most preachers from speaking before a congregation of strangers. But not Paul. He spoke God's truth, and the Galatians, believing what he said, received him "as an angel of God, as Christ Jesus Himself."

Apparently, a spiritual bond formed between them that transcended human attraction. The Galatians saw Paul as God's messenger and as Christ's ambassador.[5] Consequently, they responded to him with wholehearted affection. Their devotion stemmed from "a sense of blessing" they had. They understood that by God's providential ordering of Paul's circumstances, they had in their midst an apostle deeply committed to truth and selflessly dedicated to their spiritual welfare.[6] The Galatians were so blessed by his ministry that they bore the "trial" of his repulsive illness without complaint.

But something happened to that sense of blessing, and Paul asked them pointblank what it was. There was a time, he recalled, when they would have done anything in their power to relieve his suffering, even plucking out their own eyes and giving them to him.[7] But they no longer held him in such high regard. Although his deep commitment to truth and selfless concern for their welfare had not changed, their devotion to him had clearly waned.

Paul knew the answer to the question he asked them. He knew they had been courted by charlatans and bewitched by their teaching. He knew they had foolishly changed their allegiance without careful thought. He knew they were in danger and unaware of their peril. And he loved them too much to walk away in dejected defeat. Instead, he intensified his appeal by contrasting his true shepherd's heart to the self-serving motives of Judaizers.

## How to Evaluate Shepherds

### *(Galatians 4:16–20)*

I was genuinely converted to Christianity while attending a church that taught a lot of false doctrine. Concerned Christian friends began giving me tapes and books filled with sound biblical teaching, and I soon had a big problem. There were major discrepancies between the teaching contained in those tapes and books and the teaching I heard at church. For a while I tried to ignore my big problem by attributing the discrepancies to "semantics" or "perspective." But I was not able to do that for very long. It soon became evident that the two brands of teaching I was receiving were contradictory and could not be reconciled. I would have to choose one or the other.

The Galatians were in a similar, though not identical, predicament when they received Paul's letter. Unlike me, they had come to faith under true doctrine and were later duped by false teachers. But like me, they had come to the point of choosing one or the other. How do poor, confused laypersons make such a choice? What criteria should we use to evaluate shepherds?

Galatians 4:16–20 gives us an infallible standard: Paul's example of faithfulness to God's revealed truth and deep concern for the spiritual welfare of those under his care.

So have I become your enemy by telling you the truth? They eagerly seek you, not commendably, but they wish to shut you out so that you will seek them. But it is good always to be eagerly sought in a commendable manner, and not only when I am present with you. My children, with whom I am again in labor until Christ is formed in you—but I could wish to be present with you now and to change my tone, for I am perplexed about you.

Do you recall what we learned about rhetorical questions in lesson 4? If so, you probably sensed that Paul's question in verse 16 was not a query so much as a point maker. The point was that Paul had gone to great lengths to tell the Galatians the truth—the truth of the gospel and the truth about their own foolishness. He did that with their best interests at heart and without regard for personal consequences. Thus the answer to his question was patently obvious. Such behavior did not make him their enemy. It made him their truest friend.

The Judaizers, on the other hand, had eagerly sought out the Galatians in order to "shut them out" so the Galatians would seek them. Commentators offer various suggestions regarding what the Judaizers wanted to shut the Galatians out of, but they generally agree that the intent was to dominate the Galatians to the point of exercising exclusive influence over them. Today we might describe them as "control freaks" and recognize in them an enduring tactic used by cults and false teachers down through the centuries. One of the very best ways to bewitch gullible people is to cut them off from true friends who persistently tell them the truth.

Paul assured the Galatians that he would not mind their being pursued by faithful teachers with honorable motives, but could not idly watch them being captivated by those whose doctrine would harm them. He appealed to them as "my children"—using a Greek word that expresses special affection—and portrayed himself as a mother in the distressing position of having to give birth to the same baby twice. He thought they had been successfully birthed into the family of God, but now he was "again in labor" until Christ was formed in them.

He could not rest assured in the reality of their new birth until he saw conclusive evidence of their transformation. He was looking for them to "lay aside the old self . . . be renewed in the spirit of [their] mind[s], and put on the new self, which in the likeness of God has been created in righteousness and holiness of the truth" (Ephesians 4:22–24). He was looking for evidence that they had "laid aside the old self with its evil practices, and . . . put on the new self who is being renewed to a true knowledge according to the image of the One who created [them]—a renewal in which . . . Christ is all, and in all" (Colossians 3:9–11).

Paul earnestly desired that the Galatians be justified before God, united with Christ, and zealous for the good works that would glorify God and His Son Jesus Christ. He longed to be with them so he could "sanctify them in truth" *face to face* instead of in writing. He confessed that he was perplexed about them—at his wit's end, not sure what they were thinking or why they were straying.

As we read this part of his letter, we sense his frustration at not being able to correct the Galatians in person. So much can be communicated by the touch of a hand or the look in an eye. Paul seems acutely aware of the limitations of letters in situations like these. But he had no choice. Obviously providentially hindered from being with them, he picked up his pen and pastored long-distance. He wrote to form Christ in them—to teach, reprove, correct, and instruct in all wisdom, according to God's infallible truth, devoting his whole heart to their best interests, making their spiritual welfare his highest priority.

Paul models the kind of shepherd you and I should be following. He could say without hesitation (and did on numerous occasions), "Follow me, as I follow Christ." Paul was, admittedly, not a perfect pastor, but he came pretty close. As we make decisions about whom we will follow in our Christian walk, let's evaluate shepherds by the infallible standards Paul reflects in his letters. Let's resist the temptation to judge leaders by their appearance, mannerisms, speaking ability, availability, and demeanor. Let's follow those who are thoroughly committed to God's revealed truth, those who will labor to form Christ in us, those who will devote their whole hearts to our best interests, those who will make our spiritual welfare their highest priority.

## Notes

1. Paul Lee Tan, *Encyclopedia of 7700 Illustrations: Signs of the Times* (Rockville, Md: Assurance, 1979), 983.

2. Timothy George, *An Exegetical and Theological Exposition of Galatians*, The New American Commentary (Nashville: Broadman and Holman, 1994), 332.

3. See lesson 7.

4. Commentators vary widely in their understanding of the phrase "You have done me no wrong." My explanation of the phrase has come from reading the passage over and over in the context of Galatians 4:1–20 and asking

myself why this statement appears at this point in his argument. I may be wrong, but this is my best understanding now.

5. Commentators spill buckets of ink trying to identify Paul's illness and determine precisely how it affected his travel plans in Galatia. The discussions are fascinating, but not entirely relevant to the point we are emphasizing in this lesson. If you are interested, by all means read the commentators, but for the purposes of our lesson, simply keep in mind that Paul's disease produced disgusting symptoms and that it may have necessitated an altered route or longer stays in certain Galatian towns. Paul's message was so powerful that it completely overshadowed the natural revulsion the people would have had for his symptoms as well as the prevalent belief in those days that disease reflected the disfavor of the gods. And, of course, those who believed Paul's message would have been grateful to God for using Paul's illness as the means of bringing them the gospel.

6. Keep in mind that the word *angel* means "messenger" and that an ambassador represents the one sending him with the full authority of the one sending him. Although a few commentators see a reference to Acts 14:8–18 in this passage, most (with whom I agree) believe Paul is using these phrases as a reference to his apostolic commissioning and authority to preach God's truth.

7. Some commentators suggest that Paul's words here support the idea that Paul's illness was a severe eye disease. Others point out that in the ancient world, the eyes were considered one's most cherished possession, and conclude

that Paul's statement is simply a graphic depiction of the Galatians' great devotion to him.

E X E R C I S E S

1. List several character traits of a good pastor.

2. How does good pastoring resemble good parenting?

3. How were Paul and the Galatians "like each other."

4. What was the basis of the Galatians' initial fondness for Paul? How does Paul's reminder of their initial fondness for him strengthen his appeal to them?

5. Compare Paul's "shepherding technique" with that of the Judaizers. Which is more honoring to God and beneficial to those under the shepherd's care? Explain.

6. Reread Galatians and list verses that particularly reflect Paul's earnest desires for his readers. (Every verse in the letter reflects his earnest desires in a sense, so you can't get this wrong! But don't list every verse. Select those you believe reflect his desires most clearly and specifically.)

7. What evidence suggests that Christ is being formed in a professing believer?

8. Rewrite the facetious sketch at the beginning of this lesson so that it is more serious in tone and reflects the attributes and behavior of a faithful pastor who is committed to the truth of God's Word and devoted to the spiritual welfare of those under his care.

APPLICATION

1. This week review previous memory verses and begin memorizing one or more of the following Scripture passages:

2 Corinthians 3:18

Ephesians 4:14–16

Colossians 1:28–29

2. This week in your prayer time, choose one or more of Paul's letters and read them slowly and carefully, paying particular attention to how Paul's pastoral heart is reflected in them. List several pastors, chaplains, elders, and teachers you know personally and pray for each one by name. Thank God for calling them into ministry, for equipping and sustaining them to serve, and for helping them to remain faithful to their call. Ask God to deepen each man's desire to know Scripture deeply and to effectively meet the spiritual needs of those under his care. Pray for any particular needs of which you are aware. Then write an encouraging note to each one on your list.

3. In his letters, Paul frequently exhorted his readers to imitate him or to follow his example (1 Corinthians 4:16; 11:1; Galatians 4:12; Philippians 3:17; 4:9; 1 Thessalonians 1:6; 2 Thessalonians 3:7, 9). His words were not addressed exclusively to ordained pastors, elders, and deacons. He also intended them to be read and applied by rank-and-file laypeople. Many of us in that category are taken aback by his boldness and admit to deep reluctance to "follow his example" by encouraging others to imitate us! Derek Thomas sheds some insightful light on our plight: "We are often reluctant to draw attention to ourselves—not out of constraints of modesty so much as a haunting realization that our sanctification is so pitifully unChristlike and immature. Our recoil at Paul's audacity may be the projection of guilt due to our lack of Christian growth and maturity" (Derek Thomas, *Let's*

*Study Galatians* [Carlisle, Pa.: Banner of Truth, 2004], 112). Scot McKnight helps us overcome this reluctance by suggesting that we closely examine precisely what it was about Paul that he was asking others to imitate (Scot McKnight, *Galatians*, The NIV Application Commentary [Grand Rapids, Mich.: Zondervan, 1995], 218). Of course, we cannot imitate his authority as an apostle, but there are many characteristics of Paul that, if imitated, would help us grow in grace and knowledge of Jesus Christ and be better examples for those we influence. Read the following passages carefully and make a list of personal attributes Paul encourages his readers to imitate: 1 Corinthians 4:1–16; 10:31–11:1; Galatians 4:8–20; Philippians 3:2–21; 4:4–9; 1 Thessalonians 1:1–10; 2 Thessalonians 3:4–15. Pick two of these attributes and make a detailed plan of action that will help you follow Paul's example in these areas. As soon as following his example in these areas becomes "habitual" for you, chose two more attributes to work on. Continue in this manner until you have completed your list.

## DIGGING DEEPER

Paul's relationship with the Galatians, reflected in his letter to them, has been called a perfect illustration of what he taught about love in 1 Corinthians 13. Read 1 Corinthians 13 carefully, noting how Paul describes love in that passage. Then read Galatians carefully, noting particular examples of Paul's speech, attitudes, and behavior toward the Galatians that illustrate his teaching about love. If you have time, do the same thing with one or more of Paul's other letters. What does this exercise teach you about Paul's effectiveness as a pastor, a leader, and a mentor? How might you imitate his example to become more effective in evangelizing the lost and discipling other believers?

*Primary Passage*
GALATIANS 4:21–5:1

*Supplementary Passages*
GENESIS 12:1–3; 15:1–17:8; 18:1–15; 21:1–21; 25:12–18
ISAIAH 54:1–5
MATTHEW 3:1–9
JOHN 8:31–47
ACTS 15:1–11
ROMANS 4:1–25; 9:6–9, 30–33; 10:8–13; 15:8–13
1 CORINTHIANS 10:1–6
2 CORINTHIANS 3:4–18
PHILIPPIANS 3:17–21
HEBREWS 11:8–12

Before reading the lesson material, please read the primary
Scripture passage listed above and as many of the supplementary passages as time allows. Then briefly summarize in
your notebook what you have read. (Do not go into detail.
Limit your summary to a brief description of the people,
events, and/or ideas discussed in the passages.)

# Born Free

*Religion can keep you from God. It can become the substitute—and not a very good one—for a relationship with God himself. Something about institutionalized Christianity (as necessary as it is) will kill your freedom, if you aren't careful.* —STEVE BROWN

F or ten years, Princess Elisa Carolina Casaretto Borghese lived as a virtual prisoner in her own palatial residence in Genoa, Italy. Heiress to a million dollars, the seventy-seven-year-old Princess was mesmerized by a certain Baron Waldemar Von Hoyningenp-Huene, who along with an Italian woman, moved into the Princess's apartment. The Princess was forced to live miserably in a servant room adjoining the apartment, a small, dirty place without even an electric light.

When neighbors began to notice the Princess's threadbare clothes and torn stockings and to hear her beg for a little money, they reported the matter to the police, who then uncovered the whole strange story. The Princess told them, "At first they moved into my home as friends and then became strangers, and I didn't know how to get free."

She gradually came to believe that she was poor and that she had to do whatever the baron said, but she couldn't explain why she felt so intimidated. Once back in her apartment, the old Princess sought to begin life anew. "Now that I know they were evil, I can't stop wondering how they got control of me. It's been a nightmare, and now I am free."[1]

The Princess's story strikes us as sad and tragic, doesn't it? Why is that, do you think? Was it simply because she went from wealth to poverty? Comfort to misery? Plenty to want? Surely not. Lots of folks weather such storms of life, and their stories strike us as heroic and uplifting. The Princess's story breaks our hearts not because of her circumstances alone. It grieves us because she was duped by self-serving charlatans into willingly trading inherited privilege for pointless bondage. Does that sound familiar? By now it should.

The Galatians to whom Paul wrote were on the brink of doing precisely what the Princess had done. Born into God's family through their union with Christ, they were free to enjoy great inherited privilege. But self-serving Judaizers had moved into their apartment and somehow convinced them that they were born to bondage. Thankfully, concerned neighbors reported their perilous situation more quickly than did those of the Princess!

Paul wrote as soon as he heard of their plight. As believers in Christ, he told them, they were children of promise, spiritual descendants of Abraham through Sarah, not Hagar. They were "born free," not to bondage. And they were, consequently, responsible to live in accordance with their true identity. In Galatians 4:21–5:1, Paul reassured them (again!) of their standing in Christ and called them to "stand firm" in their freedom by "casting out" the deceivers with their enslaving false doctrines.

## A Difficult Rescue

### *(Galatians 4:21–28)*

Paul's letter to the Galatians was, in essence, a rescue effort—a rescue effort made difficult by the Galatians' apparent contentment in their captivity. Much like the Princess Borghese, they had been convinced that they were something they were not and had settled into living according to that false identity. Before Paul could deliver them from unwarranted bondage, he had to persuade them of who they were in reality—free children of promise, heirs of God, who should live accordingly.

Paul knew that their chains had been forged in the fires of deceptive teaching. And he also knew that those chains were no match for "the sword of the Spirit, which is the word of God." In Galatians 4:21–28, he deals a death blow to the Judaizers' false doctrine by summing up his defense of justification by grace alone through faith alone in Christ alone with an Old Testament illustration aimed at convincing the Galatians of their true identity.

> Tell me, you who want to be under law, do you not listen to the
> law? For it is written that Abraham had two sons, one by the

bondwoman and one by the free woman. But the son by the bondwoman was born according to the flesh, and the son by the free woman through the promise. This is allegorically speaking, for these women are two covenants: one proceeding from Mount Sinai bearing children who are to be slaves; she is Hagar. Now this Hagar is Mount Sinai in Arabia and corresponds to the present Jerusalem, for she is in slavery with her children. But the Jerusalem above is free; she is our mother. For it is written,

> "Rejoice, barren woman who does not bear;
> Break forth and shout, you who are not in labor;
> For more numerous are the children of the desolate
> Than of the one who has a husband."

And you brethren, like Isaac, are children of promise.

Paul's tactics are deftly disarming. He does not raise the Galatians' defensive hackles by smashing them over the head with their misunderstanding of truth. Instead, he challenges them to develop their understanding more fully. "You want to be under the law?" he asks, in effect. "Well, let's see what the law you want to be under says about that."

Paul used the word "law" in two senses here—the first in a limited sense to refer to the law given to Moses on Sinai, and the second in a broader sense to refer to the first five books of the Bible.[2] He was advising the Galatians that the law given to Moses cannot stand alone. It is an aspect of God's revealed plan and purpose that can only be understood and applied rightly within its historical and spiritual context.

Paul's words in this passage suggest that the Judaizers had taken advantage of the Galatians' understandably scant knowledge of how God's plan and purpose were revealed in Jewish history. We do not know precisely what the Judaizers taught the Galatians, but Paul's response implies that they may have drawn false conclusions from partial truth.

It certainly appears that the Judaizers *accurately* affirmed that the Jews were the "legitimate" physical descendants of Abraham through his wife Sarah and son Isaac—and then *inaccurately* concluded that Jews alone could lay claim to God's redemptive promise. Such a spurious argument would have supported their assertion that Gentiles, who were not legitimate physical descendants of Abraham, could receive God's promise only by "becoming Jews"—accepting circumcision and following prescribed ceremonial rituals.

Many commentators suggest that Paul was indeed countering such nefarious doctrine when he told the Galatians "the whole truth" and drew conclusions that differed dramatically from those of the Judaizers. If you have studied the Gospels, you are probably aware that Paul was not plowing new ground here. John the Baptist and Jesus Christ had already warned the Jews not to trust in their fleshly lineage because *spiritual* descent from Abraham is what really matters (Matthew 3:7–10; John 8:33–44). Paul, in this passage, simply reiterated that teaching and went on to explain that spiritual descent is not tied to physical heritage. He assured his readers that spiritual descent from Abraham belongs to those who share Abraham's God-given faith, not his "legitimate" genes.

Paul affirmed that Abraham did indeed have two sons, one by the slave woman and one by the free woman. The son of the slave woman (Ishmael) did not become Abraham's physical heir, but the son of the free woman (Isaac) did. However, the factor determining which boy would be the legitimate heir was not necessarily whom they called "Mom." It was, in fact, the manner by which each was conceived.

Abraham fathered Ishmael "according to the flesh"—according to his own plans, in his own strength, and within the realm of human ability. He fathered Isaac "through the promise"—in dependence upon God's Word, in the power of God's Spirit, and outside the realm of human ability. Ishmael was a child of works-righteousness born into slavery. Isaac was a child of faith born into freedom.

Paul used this historical incident from the life of Abraham as an allegorical[3] illustration to summarize powerfully his defense of justification by faith alone. The mothers of the two boys, Hagar and Sarah, represented two incompatible ways of relating to God. Hagar, the mother of the son of works-righteousness, represented God's law given at Sinai misconstrued as the way to right standing with God. Paul said that Hagar and her descendants—those who did not pursue righteousness by faith, "but as though it were by works" (Romans 9:31–32)—were in slavery. They were bound to a futile legalism that could never be a means of earning favor with God. Sarah, the mother of the son of faith, represented God's gospel of grace through faith in Jesus Christ. She was the mother of "numerous . . . children" from all the world's nations who look to God in faith for redemption and blessing (Jerusalem above).[4]

Paul reminded his brethren in Galatia that they were among those who had trusted in Christ for their salvation. Despite their fleshly lineage, they were, "like Isaac, children of promise." As such, they possessed great inherited privilege, but tragically, they were in danger of squandering it. If they accepted the false doctrine of Judaizers, they would be no better off than the Princess Borghese—submitting themselves to pointless bondage. Paul calls them to acknowledge their heritage, denounce their oppressors, and live in accordance with their true identity.

## Another Masterful Transition

### *(Galatians 4:28–5:1)*

Do you recall from lesson 3 that Paul was a master of the delicate art of transition? If so, stick another gold star inside your book cover and get ready to watch him do it again. Paul's adroit use of transition in this letter is easy to miss simply because he does it so well. As he defended three essential elements of God's gospel of grace (apostolic authority, justification, and sanctification), he moved from one to the other so smoothly that we hardly notice his change of subject.

In Galatians 2:11–21, Paul's transition from affirming his apostolic authority to upholding justification by grace alone through faith alone in Christ alone was essentially seamless. And in Galatians 4:28–5:1, he moved just as deftly from upholding justification to portraying sanctification as the pursuit of holiness in the power of the Holy Spirit for the glory of God.

> And you brethren, like Isaac, are children of promise. But as at that time he who was born according to the flesh persecuted him who was born according to the Spirit, so it is now also. But what does the Scripture say?
>
> > "Cast out the bondwoman and her son,
> > For the son of the bondwoman shall not be an heir with the son of the free woman."

So then, brethren, we are not children of a bondwoman, but of the free woman. It was for freedom that Christ set us free; therefore keep standing firm and do not be subject again to a yoke of slavery.

Notice that Paul began this section by describing his brethren as children of promise—justified sinners who have been guaranteed an inheritance because of their union with Christ. Then he explained that they will attract persecution *because of who they are*—and should respond with behavior that glorifies God.

Paul transitioned from justification to sanctification in Galatians 4:28–5:1 by grounding his commands to live for God's glory in the truth he had taught about the transforming power of justification. Since his Galatian brethren had been indwelt by God's Spirit and set free for freedom, they should stand firm in their faith and refuse to submit to pointless bondage.

Just as Isaac had been persecuted by Ishmael, Paul's brethren in Galatia were persecuted by Judaizers. And because they misunderstood their identity as children of God, they foolishly cowered before them. The deceivers in their midst proudly laid claim to Abraham's "legitimate genes," although they did not share his faith. The Judaizers audaciously added slavish terms to God's promise, although they could not lay claim to that promise themselves. Paul told the Galatians not to put up with such utter nonsense. "Follow the example of Father Abraham," he advised them in essence. "And toss them out on their ears!"

Paul exhorted his brethren to acknowledge and stand firm in their true identity—children of the free woman, not of the bondwoman. Their salvation in Christ had released them from the law's curse and broken their bondage to futile legalistic attempts to curry favor with God. Their faith in Christ's work on their behalf freed them to live righteously in the power of His indwelling Spirit for the glory of God. Faith had accomplished what the law could not do: It made them sons of God, children of promise, heirs-by-right and heirs-in-fact of great standing and privilege.

Using a military term meaning to keep alert, stick together, be strong, and resist attack, Paul urged them to "stand firm" against the efforts of Judaizers who desired to bring them back under bondage. They had been set free "for freedom" and were now able, responsible, and indescribably blessed to obey God in the power of His Holy Spirit, not through legalistic rule-keeping.

Their sanctification—fulfilling their chief end of glorifying and enjoying God—would occur as they lived righteous lives *in His strength*, not their own. Their Spirit-empowered obedience would effectively mirror God's righteousness and proclaim His excellencies to those around them (Matthew 5:16; Ephesians 2:10; Titus 2:11–14; 1 Peter 2:9). Faith in God's grace had justified them, and faith in God's grace would sanctify them.

In the remainder of his letter to the Galatians, Paul will affirm that the obedience that most glorifies God does not flow from stringent, legalistic self-effort, but from the liberating and empowering presence of His Holy Spirit. He will describe all that being "set free for freedom" entails. He will encourage his readers not to squander their inherited privilege. He will call us to pursue holiness in the strength of God's might for the display of His glory. And he will affirm that we do that by making "visible in the earthly realm of . . . human existence what God has already declared and sealed in the divine verdict of justification."[5]

# Notes

1. Adapted from "It's Been a Nightmare," in Paul Lee Tan, *Encyclopedia of 7700 Illustrations: Signs of the Times* (Rockville, Md: Assurance, 1979), 603–4.

2. The first five books of the Bible are referred to as the "Pentateuch," a term that means "five-volumed." The Jews have traditionally referred to these books as "The Book of the Law," or simply "The Law" ("Pentateuch," *Nelson's New Illustrated Bible Dictionary*, ed., Ronald F. Youngblood [Nashville: Nelson, 1986], 962).

3. Allegories in Scripture make sincere Bible students nervous. That's because sincere Bible students know that fanciful "allegorical exegesis" butchers the clear meaning of Scripture. The sincere Bible students who wrote most of the commentaries I read seemed so nervous, in fact, that they went to great lengths to affirm that Galatians 4:22–27 is not really an allegory at all, but simply a "type" or an "analogy." And their heroic efforts made me very nervous. I was left wondering why Paul, writing under the inspiration of God's Holy Spirit, would call something an allegory when it is not. A few brave commentators, with whom I choose to stand, accepted Paul's statement at face value and helpfully explained that Paul was not *exegeting Scripture allegorically* here, but *speaking allegorically* to make a point. He responsibly exegeted the Genesis passage for what it is, historical narrative, and then used that historical narrative allegorically to illustrate spiritual truth about justification.

4. The quote Paul uses in Galatians 4:27 in reference to Sarah is taken from Isaiah 54:1, which likens Jerusalem to a barren widow who had no children to care for her in

her old age, but whose situation has been reversed by the sovereign intervention of God. The similarity between Jerusalem's situation and that of both Sarah and believers in Christ is fairly obvious. The desperate situation of God's chosen people, in all ages, will be reversed—as a result of the "crushing" of God's servant, Jesus Christ (Isaiah 53).

5. Timothy George, *An Exegetical and Theological Exposition of Galatians*, The New American Commentary (Nashville: Broadman and Holman, 1994), 352.

## E x e r c i s e s

<u>REVIEW</u>

1. What made Paul's efforts to rescue the Galatians so difficult? What did he have to do in order to rescue them? How did he do it?

2. How is descent from Abraham related to salvation by grace alone through faith alone in Christ alone?

3. What factor was most important in determining which of Abraham's two sons (Ishmael and Isaac) would be his legitimate heir?

4. How do Hagar and Sarah represent two incompatible ways of relating to God in Paul's allegorical illustration?

5. Describe Paul's masterful transition from justification to sanctification in the verses we studied in this lesson.

6. What does Paul say we who are children of God should do because we have been "set free for freedom"? What are some ways you might begin today to obey Paul's command?

7. Based on what you have learned so far in Galatians, explain how "religion can keep you from God. . . . if you aren't careful."

## APPLICATION

1. This week review previous memory verses and begin memorizing one or more of the following Scripture passages:

   John 8:31–32, 36
   Romans 6:16–18
   Galatians 5:1

2. This week in your prayer time, use John 8:31–36; Romans 3:20–26; 6:1–23; 2 Corinthians 3:4–6; and Galatians 5:1 to help you thank God for your freedom in Christ and to seek His help through His Spirit to guard your freedom carefully and use it responsibly.

3. Christians have been transformed by God's indwelling Spirit, and therefore delight in proclaiming His excellencies through obedience to His commands. Thus, we are not "free from the Law" in the sense that we are free to disobey God. Rather, we are "free from the Law" in the sense that we do not *rely on our obedience* to the law for right standing with God. Although we glorify God by obeying His commands in the power of His Spirit, we *rely on Christ's obedience* to the law imputed to us as the basis of our acceptance with God. Tim Keller, in his study of Galatians, says that maintaining this distinction between our obedience and our acceptance frees us from the crippling sense of guilt and inadequacy that hinders effective Christian service. He goes on to describe four kinds of people:

***Those who obey the law and rely on it:*** These people tend to be smug, self-righteous, and pharisaical. They are sure they are right with God because they do so many holy and righteous things, but they also struggle with insecure doubts that they are not doing enough. They are inclined to be touchy and very sensitive to any form of criticism.

***Those who disobey the law and rely on it:*** These people are bound by a strong work-righteousness conscience, which they consistently violate. Although they tend to be highly tolerant of other folk's sins, they are guilt-ridden most of the time. They are susceptible to mood swings and usually avoid religious topics as much as possible.

***Those who disobey the law and do not rely on it:*** These people have discarded the law of God as a standard for their behavior and established their own standards, which they can and do live by. They tend to be intellectually secular; drawn to relativistic, vague spirituality; and given to a strong liberal sense of self-righteousness.

***Those who obey the law but do not rely on it:*** These people understand God's gospel of grace and live in the freedom of it. They obey the law out of grateful joy springing from assurance of their right standing with God through the work of Christ Jesus. They tend to be happy, content, and effective in service to their Lord.

Keller affirms that genuine Christians should be in the last category, but that most of us lean toward categories 1, 2, or 3. To the extent that we lean toward those first three categories, we impoverish ourselves spiritually and fall short of our high calling in Christ (Tim Keller, *Paul's*

*Letter to the Galatians: Living in Line with the Truth of the Gospel, Leader's Guide* [New York: Redeemer Presbyterian Church, 2002]. Leader's notes for question #1, lesson 9, "Grace to the Barren." Downloaded from Redeemer Presbyterian Church Web site [www.redeemer.com]. No page numbers).

Prayerfully examine your thoughts, words, and actions for a period of one month with the intent of discovering which of Keller's four categories best reflects your relationship with the Lord. List specific thought patterns, speech patterns, and behavior patterns that suggest your individual tendency. Ask members of your family, close friends, and your spiritual leaders (pastor, elders, deacons, teachers) to help you analyze your tendency. If you are inclined toward one of Keller's first three categories, think back over what you have already learned from Paul in the book of Galatians. What specific applications of what you have learned will help you live more consistently within Keller's last category? What specific thought, speech, and behavior patterns do you need to change? How will you make these changes? When will you begin making them? Who will hold you accountable for making them?

## DIGGING DEEPER

What does it mean to be "free in Christ"? Study the following Scripture passages seeking to understand what Christians have been "freed from" and what we have been "freed to." When you have completed your study, write a description of "Christian freedom." Include in your description a discussion of how Christians should responsibly live in accordance with their true identity.

Luke 4:16–19; John 8:31–36; Acts 13:38–39; 15:1–29; Romans 3:19–26; 4:23–25; 5:1–2, 12–19; 6:1–23; 7:1–4, 24; 8:1–4, 20–23; 1 Corinthians 7:21–23, 32–35; 9:1, 19–23; 15:53–58; 2 Corinthians 3:4–18; Galatians 2:16–21; 3:13–14, 21, 28–29; 4:1–9, 26–31; 5:1–13, 18–25; Ephesians 1:3–21; 2:4–10; 3:20–21; 5:8; 6:10–18; Philippians 1:6; 2:12–16; 4:4–9, 13, 19; Colossians 2:6–15; 2 Timothy 1:6–14; 2:15–16; Titus 2:11–14; Hebrews 2:14–18; 4:12–16; 9:11–15; 10:19–25; 13:5–6, 15, 20–21; James 1:5; 2:12; 4:6–10; 1 Peter 1:3–5; 2:9–12, 16; 2 Peter 1:2–4; 1 John 1:5–9; 2:3; 3:1–3; 4:4, 7–21; 5:4–5, 14–15; Revelation 21:1–7; 22:12–17.

*Primary Passage*
GALATIANS 5:2–15

*Supplementary Passages*
LEVITICUS 19:18
DEUTERONOMY 23:1
ISAIAH 29:13–14
JEREMIAH 23:16–24
MATTHEW 16:6; 18:5–7
LUKE 10:25–37
JOHN 8:31–36
ACTS 15:6–11
ROMANS 6:15–23; 8:1–39; 9:30–33; 13:8–10
1 CORINTHIANS 1:18–25; 7:17–20
PHILIPPIANS 1:6
COLOSSIANS 3:5–11
1 THESSALONIANS 1:2–5
JAMES 1:21–25; 2:8

Before reading the lesson material, please read the primary
Scripture passage listed above and as many of the supplementary passages as time allows. Then briefly summarize in
your notebook what you have read. (Do not go into detail.
Limit your summary to a brief description of the people,
events, and/or ideas discussed in the passages.)

# Getting Back
# on the Right Road

*The divergence from the straight road is often so very small
that he who has abandoned it may easily for a time persuade
himself that he is still [pursuing] it.* —JOHN BROWN

When my husband Frank was in college, he and his
Grandpa Van decided to take a road trip to Kansas
to visit some relatives. To conserve as much time as possible
for visiting, they chose to leave late in the evening, right after
their Friday night bowling league. Frank had been in classes all
day and was tired. But Grandpa Van had taken the day off and
napped, so he volunteered to drive while Frank slept.

Grandpa Van had not done much long-distance driving,
so before drifting off to dreamland, Frank carefully reviewed
with him the route they had marked on their trusty roadmap:

northeast from Albuquerque, across the corner of Texas and the Oklahoma panhandle into Kansas, and then through Dodge City into Great Bend. Confident that the older man knew where he was going, Frank stretched out and dozed off.

When he awoke, sunlight was illuminating some beautiful scenery that did not look at all like Texas, or Oklahoma, or Kansas. "Where are we?" Frank mumbled, to which Grandpa replied, "Should be gettin' pert near Kansas." Frank was, frankly, skeptical and starting looking for clues as to their real whereabouts. A few minutes later, his suspicions were confirmed when he spotted a road sign announcing that they were, in fact, "gettin' pert near" Lamar, Colorado.

Frank asked Grandpa Van a few relevant questions and found out that he had come to a slight fork in the road a few hours back and taken "the best lookin' option." By the time Frank woke up, they were a good five hours off course. My poor husband then faced the unenviable challenge of persuading his misguided Grandpa that the road they were on would not get them to their desired destination. If they wanted to visit family in Kansas, they would have to follow the map Grandpa had ignored.

The apostle Paul faced essentially the same challenge when he took pen in hand to write to the Galatians. His straying brethren had chosen "the best lookin' option" of legalistic false teaching and wandered severely off course. Paul knew that the only way to get them back on the right road was to re-fix their attention on the inspired map of God's truth they had unwisely neglected.

In Galatians 5:2–15, he affirmed that they were indeed on the wrong road, asserted that their detour resulted from ignoring their well-marked map, and reminded them that there was only one way to their desired destination.

## You Are on the Wrong Road

### *(Galatians 5:2–6)*

The Galatians, much like Grandpa Van, had cruised along unaware that they were on the wrong road—until Paul dropped this mini-bombshell on them.

> Behold I, Paul, say to you that if you receive circumcision, Christ will be of no benefit to you. And I testify again to every man who receives circumcision, that he is under obligation to keep the whole Law. You have been severed from Christ, you who are seeking to be justified by law; you have fallen from grace. For we through the Spirit, by faith, are waiting for the hope of righteousness. For in Christ Jesus neither circumcision nor uncircumcision means anything, but faith working through love. (5:2–6)

Paul wielded the big stick of his apostolic authority to get their attention. "Look here! Listen to me," he said in effect. "I, Paul the apostle, know where that road you're on leads, and take it from me, you don't want to go there."

Paul had already shown them that the doctrine of the Judaizers differed very little from the pagan practices from which they had been redeemed through faith in Christ Jesus (Galatians 4:1–11).[1] Both were "elemental things of the world" that held unbelievers in bondage. Faith in Christ freed Jew and Gentile alike from enslavement to all forms of legalistic religious practices. So, trading one form for another was absolutely ridiculous. But that was precisely what the Galatians had been duped into doing.

They had stepped on the wrong road of legalistic false doctrine by observing "days and months and seasons and years." And now they were dangerously close to accepting circumcision. Paul said that if they did, "Christ [would] be of no benefit" to them. That next step on the wrong road would obligate them to fulfill the whole law, cut them off from Christ, and remove them from the realm of God's grace.

Was Paul saying, as some have suggested, that they were one step away from forfeiting their salvation? No, he was not. Paul argued elsewhere, under the inspiration of God's Holy Spirit, that those whom God justifies He also glorifies, that no one can bring a charge against God's elect, and that nothing can separate Christians from the love of God, which is in Christ Jesus (Romans 8:30–39).

Rightly understanding these frequently misunderstood verses requires us to consider them within their context. In the verses immediately preceding these, Paul transitioned from his defense of justification as coming by grace alone through faith alone in Christ alone to his description of sanctification as the pursuit of holiness in the power of the Holy Spirit for the glory of God. He called the Galatians to live out their salvation in the freedom for which Christ had freed them. And he implored them to keep standing firm and refuse to be subject again to a yoke of slavery. In the verses to come, Paul affirmed that their "hope of righteousness" was grounded not in their works-righteousness, but in their faith in God's promise to complete the good work He had begun in them (Philippians 1:6).

Thus, Paul's remarks in Galatians 5:2–4 do not contradict other clear teaching in Scripture. Instead, they assert that our sanctification is just as gracious as is our justification. Our hope of righteousness is something we "are waiting for," not something we are working toward. Justification *graciously* freed us from sin's penalty, *graciously* is freeing us from sin's power, and *graciously* will free us from sin's presence. We were *graciously* declared righteous when we were redeemed, we are *graciously* being inclined and equipped to live righteously in this present world, and we will be *graciously* made righteous when we are glorified, fully conformed to the image of Christ.

The gracious character of our salvation does not eliminate the requirement to live righteously in this present age. Rather, it frees us to live righteously in the power of the Spirit for the glory of God. As the indwelling Spirit sets our minds on the hope of God's promise to eventually glorify us, He stimulates our desire to live righteously as we walk through this world. As He works in us to equip us to do the good works God prepared for us, our lives are characterized by *increasing* righteousness.

Such Spirit-motivated and Spirit-empowered righteousness does not seek to merit favor with God. Instead it reflects our faith in Him working through our love for Him. This is the essence of Paul's doctrine of sanctification. And it was his Spirit-inspired response to those who argued that his doctrine of grace was a fast track to licentiousness. In Galatians 5:13–26, he will affirm that "faith working through love" is, in reality, the only way to rightly obey God. John Murray captured the heart of Paul's teaching on sanctification when he explained that grace brings God's will and power together for the purpose of delivering fallen men and women "from thought and conduct that bind them to the servitude of unholiness." Grace, Murray said, is thus "deliverance from that which consists in transgression of the law."[2]

Paul understood that grace is as essential to sanctification as it is to justification. He knew that when God's grace justifies us, it also transforms us. It replaces hard hearts of stone with soft hearts of flesh that are responsive to the leading of His indwelling Spirit. And therefore it motivates and empowers joyful, God-honoring obedience in ways legalistic rule-keeping simply cannot.

But before Paul could develop that crucial subject, he had to get his misguided brethren back on the right road.

## You Ignored Your Map

### *(Galatians 5:7–12)*

Writing on Galatians in the mid-nineteenth century, Professor John Brown asserted that a primary responsibility of pastors is to believe the best about the folks in their flocks for as long they possibly can. Whenever a pastor "stands in doubt of any of those whose souls are committed to his care," Brown said, "he must not conceal his hopes while he makes known his fears."[3] John Brown was, of course, urging pastors to pattern their pastoring after that of Paul the apostle.

After alerting his wayward flock to the futility of their detour into works-righteousness, Paul admonished the Galatians as those in whom he had confidence, not as those on whom he had given up. He came alongside them to help them get back on the right road by pinpointing precisely where they went wrong, affirming his certainty that they could and would correct their course, and aiming his anger at the deceitful Judaizers, not at his misguided brethren.

> You were running well; who hindered you from obeying the truth? This persuasion did not come from Him who calls you. A little leaven leavens the whole lump of dough. I have confidence in you in the Lord that you will adopt no other view; but the one who is disturbing you will bear his judgment, whoever he is. But I, brethren, if I still preach circumcision, why am I still persecuted? Then the stumbling block of the cross has been abolished. I wish that those who are troubling you would even mutilate themselves. (5:7–12)

Frank's Grandpa Van and the Galatians both started out well on their individual journeys. And both ended up on the wrong road for analogous reasons. Grandpa Van took a wrong turn when he chose to ignore his well-marked roadmap. And the Galatians were "hindered . . . from obeying the truth" when they heeded persuasive teachers who did not speak for God.

Using a generally true and helpful proverb, Paul advised them that even a small amount of false teaching corrupts God's truth immensely. The Galatians had been foolish to believe that stirring a little works-righteousness into God's gospel of grace would enhance its effectiveness. Paul had taught them that grace and merit don't mix and that even a smidgeon of legalism dena-tures[4] God's grace. The Galatians should have examined what the Judaizers were saying against the standard of Paul's inspired teaching. They wandered off-track when they chose to ignore the well-marked doctrinal map he had left them.

Paul was confident that as soon as they understood where they had gone wrong, they would do what was needed to get back on course. Paul's faith in them sprang from His knowledge of God. He believed God had rescued his Galatian brethren from the kingdom of darkness and transferred them to the kingdom of His beloved Son. Paul was therefore sure that they would not be separated from the love of God in Christ Jesus, even though they might wander around in confusion occasionally.

He had no such assurance about the Judaizers, however. They were guilty of leading God's children astray and, if they failed to repent, faced a judgment Jesus had likened to being tied to a millstone and hurled into the sea (Matthew 18:6). But that is not all the Judaizers had done. Paul implied in Galatians 5:11 that they had claimed *he also* preached circumcision as neces-sary for salvation. Paul did not waste time discussing where they came up with such an absurd allegation. He simply countered their charge with caustic logic.

"If I preach circumcision as they do," he said in effect, "why am I still being persecuted? The offense of the cross that I preach—the offense that results in my being persecuted—is that it nullifies works-righteousness. The message of the cross is a huge stumbling block to legalists because it destroys their reliance upon human merit to earn favor with God. Obviously, I have not removed the stumbling block of the cross from my message by preaching circumcision—because I am still being persecuted!"

Interestingly, Paul chose not to rest his case at that point, but followed it up with some scathing sarcasm. "If the Judaizers think circumcision merits favor with God," he said in effect, "why don't they curry even more favor with Him by castrating themselves!"

Were you as shocked as I was to read those graphic words? Did you wonder why God's Holy Spirit inspired Paul to write such a distasteful sentence? If so, perhaps it will help to consider it in the light of what we learned about "elemental things of the world" in Galatians 4:1–11. If your memory is a bit fuzzy, reread those verses and pages 108–11 of lesson 7 before going on.

Many pagan religious cults in Paul's day practiced castration as part of their worship rites. They believed that such radical mutilation of the body earned favor with their false gods. Paul knew the true God prohibited such practices (Deuteronomy 23:1) and had given circumcision not as a means of earning His favor, but as a sign of His promise to Abraham. The Judaizers, however, were teaching that circumcision was a righteous act essential to salvation and right standing with God. They were pursuing salvation not "by faith, but as though it were by works."

Paul's shocking sarcasm seemed to align the Judaizers' distorted practice of circumcision with the pagan practice of castration. He said that if they did one, they may as well do the other. Both practices were based in works-righteousness. Both were "elemental things of the world" that led away from God's truth. The Galatians' detour into legalistic Judaism was taking them right back to the bondage from which they had been freed. Paul's angry outburst, although directed toward the Judaizers, was also an appeal to his brethren to wise up and not be "enslaved all over again."

## Only One Way to Your Desired Destination

### *(Galatians 5:13–15)*

The only way for the Galatians to get back on the road to their desired destination was to follow the inspired doctrinal map Paul had carefully marked for them. They could not wait for "the hope of righteousness" while cruising down the road of legalistic works-righteousness. Their inheritance lay at the end of a much different route—the way of "faith working through love."

They had been "set free for freedom" and called to "stand firm," refusing to submit to a "yoke of slavery." The road of freedom in Christ was indeed the only way to their desired destination. But it was a road they would be required to walk alertly. Paul warned them to proceed with caution, lest having escaped legalism, they fall into license.

> For you were called to freedom, brethren; only do not turn your freedom into an opportunity for the flesh, but through love serve one another. For the whole Law is fulfilled in one word, in the statement, "You shall love your neighbor as yourself." But if you bite and devour one another, take care that you are not consumed by one another. (5:13–15)

Timothy George captures the essence of Paul's warning when he says God intends for believers in this world to be "in the flesh" but not "of the flesh."[5] The Greek word translated "flesh," *sarx*, often refers to sinful human nature characterized by prideful self-righteousness and indulgent self-will.[6] The flesh is attracted to both legalism and license because both are self-centered.

Although Christians live "in the flesh" (Galatians 2:20), we have been freed from the necessity to live "of the flesh." We have been united with Christ and indwelt by His Spirit. We have been transformed into people who derive intense joy from giving God glory in everything that we do. The freedom for which we have been set free breaks the bonds of self-righteous legalism and self-indulgent license. We are "children of promise" redeemed through the work of God's Son and equipped by His Spirit to live for His glory.

Our faith in what God has done for us and in us frees us to serve one another in love. Exercising this freedom fulfills the whole law because it draws on a right relationship with God in order to relate rightly to the people around us.[7] "Faith working through love" reflects God's power at work in us to enable us to regard others as more important than ourselves (Philippians 2:3–4).

Living "in the flesh" but not "of the flesh" requires effort on our part. We remain vulnerable to fleshly temptations as we walk through this world. Paul reminded us that succumbing to them inevitably destroys the interpersonal harmony that glorifies God. Fulfilling the chief end for which we were saved requires us to walk by the Spirit so that we will not fulfill the desires of the flesh. And Paul will describe how we do that in our next lesson.

## *Notes*

1. See pages 108–11 of lesson 7.

2. John Murray, *Principles of Conduct: Aspects of Biblical Ethics* (Grand Rapids, Mich.: Eerdmans, 1957), 186.

3. John Brown, *Galatians: A Geneva Series Commentary* (1853; reprint, Carlisle, Pa.: Banner of Truth, 2001), 274.

4. See note 1 following lesson 5 to refresh your memory about how adding legalism to God's grace denatures it.

5. Timothy George, *An Exegetical and Theological Exposition of Galatians*, The New American Commentary (Nashville: Broadman and Holman, 1994), 377.

6. Ibid.

7. At first glance, it might appear that Paul, in Galatians 5:14, is contradicting Jesus' statement that fulfilling the whole Law and the Prophets rest on two commandments: loving God with all your heart, soul, and mind, and loving your neighbor as yourself. Is Paul saying that the Law is fulfilled by loving your neighbor without loving God? No. The commentators I read consistently agreed that Paul is assuming that no one is able to love their neighbor the way Scripture commands unless he or she first loves God as only a transformed child of God can through the power of the indwelling Spirit. For additional insight into Paul's meaning in this verse, tackle Digging Deeper question 1 in this lesson.

## E x e r c i s e s

### REVIEW

1. How did Paul's Galatian brethren end up on the wrong road of legalistic false doctrine?

2. What do Paul's words in Galatians 5:2–7 reveal about the nature of justification and sanctification?

3. What is our "hope of righteousness"? How does waiting for our hope of righteousness encourage us to live righteously as we walk through this world?

4. Explain in your own words the essence of Paul's doctrine of sanctification.

5. On what does Paul base his confidence that his Galatian brethren will do what is needed to get back on the right road?

6. How does freedom in Christ equip believers to live "in the flesh" but not "of the flesh"?

## APPLICATION

1. This week review previous memory verses and begin memorizing one or more of the following Scripture passages:

   Matthew 18:7
   Romans 8:14–17
   Galatians 5:13

2. This week in your prayer time, use Romans 8:1–39 to help you: (1) thank God for setting you free from the law of sin and death, (2) praise God for His glorious plan of salvation, (3) confess your failures to live in accord with who you are in Christ, and (4) seek His help in understanding how your transformation in Christ equips you to live "in the flesh" but not "of the flesh."

3. As we Christians seek to glorify God by walking worthy of our high calling in Christ, some of us are easily tempted to detour into legalism. Others of us are more likely to get tripped up by license. And some of us struggle with both

(legalistic in some areas and licentious in others). Which category best characterizes you? Are you more prone to think being a Christian means keeping a long list of rules? Do you tend to think being Christian means never having to say *I should . . .* or *I must . . .*? Or does it all depend on the issue involved? Make a list of your typical thoughts, statements, and actions that reflect your general view of what being a Christian is all about. Then analyze your list to see if you can detect a propensity toward legalism, license, or both. How will what you have learned in this lesson help you correct these tendencies so you can glorify and enjoy God more effectively?

4. List one or more specific examples of how your faith helps you love and serve others. (Keep in mind that a specific example answers the questions, who? what? when? where? and how? Thus, your examples should answer these questions: *Who* has your faith helped you love and serve? *What* did your faith help you think, say, or do for this person? *When* did it help you think, say, or do it? *Where* did this action occur? *How* did your faith help you love and serve this person?)

## DIGGING DEEPER

Read and study Luke 10:25–37; Romans 6:11–23; Romans 8:12–17; Romans 9:30–32; Romans 13:8–10; 2 Corinthians 5:11–17; Philippians 3:2–14; James 1:21–25; and James 2:8. Then use what you learn from these verses to demonstrate that Paul's words in Galatians 5:14 do not contradict Jesus' statement in Matthew 22:39.

Define, in your own words, the phrase "faith working through love." How does this phrase relate to serving one another in love?

*Primary Passage*
GALATIANS 5:16–25

*Supplementary Passages*
LEVITICUS 19:9–18
PSALM 1:1–6
ISAIAH 26:3
JEREMIAH 17:5–10
EZEKIEL 11:17–21; 36:24–32
MATTHEW 5:20–48; 7:15–23; 12:33–37; 22:37–40
MARK 7:20–23
JOHN 3:6; 12:23–26; 15:1–11
ROMANS 5:1–5; 6:1–23; 7:14–25; 8:1–4, 12–17
1 CORINTHIANS 6:9–12; 15:10, 56–58
2 CORINTHIANS 5:17; 13:5
PHILIPPIANS 2:12–16
COLOSSIANS 1:9–12; 2:6–7
JAMES 2:14–26
2 PETER 1:2–4
1 JOHN 3:4–10

Before reading the lesson material, please read the primary Scripture passage listed above and as many of the supplementary passages as time allows. Then briefly summarize in your notebook what you have read. (Do not go into detail. Limit your summary to a brief description of the people, events, and/or ideas discussed in the passages.)

# The Spirit Connection

*The Christian has the glorious privilege of living under*
*the internal guidance, restraint, and power of the Holy*
*Spirit, who energizes him to obey the will of God.*
—JOHN MACARTHUR

The British scholar and military strategist Thomas Edward
Lawrence (a.k.a. Lawrence of Arabia) gained the respect
and trust of many Arab leaders during his innovative and bold
service during World War I. Consequently, he was asked to
participate in the Paris peace talks following the war. Several

Arab leaders accompanied him to Paris, where they all stayed in the same hotel.

In the process of investigating their highly comfortable accommodations, the Arab leaders discovered that amazing amounts of water gushed into bathtubs and sinks at the simple turn of a handle attached to a faucet. Concluding that the faucets themselves somehow produced the water, the Arab leaders quickly developed a few basic plumbing skills. Deftly detaching the handles and faucets from the hotel's sinks and bathtubs, they squirreled them away in their suitcases before checking out of the hotel.

When Lawrence discovered what they had done, he had to explain the fatal flaw in their reasoning. The handles and faucets, which the Arabs believed would magically meet one of their most pressing needs, were useless when detached from a sure source of water.[1] Without that connection, the handles and faucets were unable to function as they were intended.

In much the same way, Paul developed his doctrine of sanctification for the Galatians by exposing the fatal flaw in the reasoning of those who were tempted to turn Christian freedom into "an opportunity for the flesh" (Galatians 5:13). He explained that the freedom for which they had been freed was intended to mold them into a people for God's own possession, zealous for good deeds that glorify Him (Titus 2:14). But in order to function as it was intended, Christian freedom must be connected to God's Holy Spirit.

## The Spirit Opposes the Flesh

### *(Galatians 5:16–18)*

Paul may have suspected that his Galatian brethren could be as easily duped by the licentious as they had been by legalists. So he proceeded to strengthen their defenses by sharpening their understanding of Christian freedom. He explained that their union with Christ freed them to fight and defeat the allure of the flesh. As believers in Christ, they were indwelt by God's Spirit and thus connected to great spiritual power. Drawing on that power empowered them to repel fleshly temptations while pursuing their chief end with joy.

> But I say, walk by the Spirit, and you will not carry out the desire of the flesh. For the flesh sets its desire against the Spirit, and the Spirit against the flesh; for these are in opposition to one another, so that you may not do the things that you please. But if you are led by the Spirit, you are not under the Law. (5:16–18)

When Paul told the Galatians, "Walk by the Spirit, and you will not carry out the desire of the flesh," he highlighted the sure link between justification and sanctification. Being adopted into God's family does more than guarantee our eternal inheritance. It also gives us His indwelling Spirit, who transforms and equips us to pursue practical holiness here in this world for the glory of God.

It would be nice if our union with Christ automatically eliminated all fleshly temptation. But, alas, it does not. My study of Scripture has led me to conclude that God planned sanctification that way because overcoming fleshly temptation in the power of His Spirit glorifies God immensely.

We glorify God when our behavior reveals, exalts, and reflects the value, significance, beauty, and majesty of God. Salvation frees us to speak, act, and think in ways that reflect God's character and nature to those around us. It does that by breaking our bondage to sin.[2] The world, the flesh, and the devil no longer have any authority to control our behavior because Jesus Christ has delivered us from their dominion. He has not yet, however, delivered us from their influence. The world, the flesh, and the devil no longer rule us, but they continue to tempt us.

Our walk on the road of freedom in Christ has been aptly compared to those tug-of-war games we all remember from schoolyard recesses and high-spirited picnics.[3] Two teams line up and pull on opposite ends of a rope. The rope moves back and forth for a while until one team overwhelms the other team's efforts. Interestingly, even when one team is clearly stronger than the other, the competition between them can become fierce—particularly when the weaker team stubbornly digs in its heels and refuses to budge.

The flesh and the Spirit pull on opposite ends of the rope of our lives. God's Spirit is, of course, the stronger contender and destined to win the ultimate victory. But the flesh is a stubborn opponent who will not concede an easy defeat. At stake is the display of God's glory through our behavior.

The flesh fights for self-exaltation, while the Holy Spirit fights for the glory of God. They battle for control of our thoughts, words, and deeds, constantly wrenching us one way or the other. When we move toward the Spirit, the flesh fires up temptation. When we lean toward the flesh, the Spirit stirs up conviction. This ongoing struggle leaves us seemingly unable to "do the things that we please." When we want to be spiritual, the flesh beguiles us with sin. When we want to be fleshly, the Spirit rains righteous rebuke on our wayward parade.

Sanctification is indeed a battle. But Paul assured the Galatians that its outcome is never in doubt for those who have been justified by faith in Christ and indwelt by God's Spirit. The transformation that always accompanies God's gracious salvation inclines and empowers His children to walk by His Spirit. Although we remain genuinely vulnerable to fleshly temptation, our lives will not be *characterized* by fleshly desire and behavior. We who are led by God's Spirit will be marked by an acute sensitivity to our own sin and an intense desire to defeat it. Our lives will reflect a clear *pattern* of increasing Christlikeness.

Paul went on to say that those who are led by the Spirit "are not under the Law." The internal restraint of God's Spirit does what the external constraint of the law has no power to do. The law rightly prescribes God's requirements, commands our obedience, and condemns our transgressions. But it cannot impart spiritual life to our fallen flesh. The law often motivates legalistic, self-exalting attempts at compliance. But it cannot be fulfilled by even the best efforts of sinners.

Only God's Spirit makes us alive in Christ Jesus, writes God's law on our hearts, and equips us to obey it. Only God's Spirit unshackles us from the law's curse. His power frees us to walk worthy of our high calling in Christ—to pursue practical holiness in the power of the Spirit for the glory of God.

## It's What's Inside That Counts

### (Galatians 5:19–23)

You have probably heard the English proverb, "You can't make a silk purse out of a sow's ear." The equivalent Spanish proverb conveys precisely the same concept with a much different image. Translated, it tells us, "Although a monkey dresses in silk, she is still a monkey."

Like most proverbs, these vivid word pictures illustrate undeniable truth—in this case, that inherent nature governs external expression. Since a sow's ear is pigskin by nature, it cannot be used to produce a silk purse. Likewise, no matter how elegantly we dress up a monkey, she will never become a fine, cultured lady. In Galatians 5:19–23, Paul explained to the Galatians that what is true of pigs and monkeys is also true of the human heart.

He affirmed the undeniable fact that unregenerate folks who are controlled by the flesh do not think, speak, or act like redeemed folks who are controlled by God's Spirit. These two groups are as different as pigskin and silk, monkeys and fine ladies. The diversity evident in their *characteristic* behavior reflects the vast difference in their true natures.

> Now the deeds of the flesh are evident, which are: immorality, impurity, sensuality, idolatry, sorcery, enmities, strife, jealousy, outbursts of anger, disputes, dissensions, factions, envying, drunkenness, carousing, and things like these, of which I forewarn you, just as I have forewarned you, that those who practice such things will not inherit the kingdom of God. But the fruit of the Spirit is love, joy, peace, patience, kindness, goodness, faithfulness, gentleness, self-control; against such things there is no law. (5:19–23)

Paul contrasted the characteristic outworking of fleshly desire with that of the indwelling Spirit by listing representative behaviors and attitudes associated with each. The fifteen "deeds of the flesh" are easily grouped into four general areas of sexual, religious, relational, and intemperate behavior. The flesh (sinful human nature characterized by prideful self-righteousness and indulgent self-will)[4] feeds sensual passions, idolatrous worship, relational discord, and lack of restraint.

Those who live under the control of the flesh are given to sexual sins (immorality) that defile them (impurity) because they cannot resist debauched wantonness (sensuality). Those who live under the control of the flesh worship false gods (idolatry) and dabble in the occult (sorcery).

Those who live under the control of the flesh are disposed toward hostility and quarrels (enmities), ill-will and bickering (strife), as well as discontentment and greedy desire for what others have (jealousy). Their behavior is marked by fits of rage and verbal violence (outbursts of anger), competitiveness and self-promotion (disputes), party-spirit and elitism (dissensions), prideful divisiveness (factions), as well as malicious rivalry (envy). Those who live under the control of the flesh are also drawn toward intoxication (drunkenness) and to the reveling it produces (carousing).

Paul warned the Galatians that "those who practice such things will not inherit the kingdom of God." Was he telling them to watch out because yielding to fleshly desires will cause them to lose their eternal inheritance? Certainly not. The Greek word translated "practice" is a present active participle that conveys the idea of ongoing, habitual activity.[5] Paul's warning reiterated what he had told the Galatians before—that those whose lives are *characterized* by such behavior "give evidence that they are not Abraham's seed and therefore will not inherit salvation."[6]

Christians are characterized by something much different, however. Those who live under the control of God's Spirit are not routinely, habitually, or customarily drawn to the deeds of the flesh. That is because we are new creations, united with Christ and indwelt by His Spirit.

Although we live "in the flesh," we are not "of the flesh." We can be enticed by fleshly desire, but we cannot be satisfied by anything that it offers. The deeds of the flesh cut cross grain to our transformation in Christ and work at cross-purposes to His indwelling Spirit. John MacArthur explains that the deeds of the flesh "are abnormal and interruptive behavior in the lives of Christians."[7] They are inconsistent with our new natures and at odds with our chief end of giving God glory.

We who live under the control of God's Spirit will, most assuredly, stumble as we strive to walk worthy of our high calling in Christ. But the general direction and character of our behavior will be, just as assuredly, colored, flavored and scented by the fruit of the Spirit. Our lives will be marked by our *love* for God and for one another, the pervasive *joy* that springs from confident hope in God's ultimate conquest of sin, and a *peace*ful sense of calm well-being deriving from a right relationship with our Creator and harmonious interactions with those around us.

We will typically manifest *patience* (steadfast obedience to God even in times of distress and trial), *kindness* (constant readiness to help others), and *goodness* (general virtue inclined toward generosity). We will be known for our *faithfulness* (trustworthiness, reliability, loyalty, and dependability), *gentleness* (strength rightly directed, mild-mannered and humble), and *self-control* (ability to exercise temperance in liberty so license is avoided).

We who walk by the Spirit will reflect "the natural produce of his gracious inward influence."[8] The fruit of the Spirit flows out of our transformation in Christ. It is not produced by legalistic adherence to a list of rules. The Spirit frees us to glorify God by inclining and empowering our hearts, minds, and wills to obey His commands.[9] J. I. Packer has said, "Holiness is the natural-ness of the spiritually risen man . . . and in pursuing holiness by obeying God, the Christian actually follows the deepest urge of his own renewed being."[10]

## Be Who You Are

### *(Galatians 5:24–25)*

Most of us, on occasion, have been advised to "just be your-self"—and perhaps have wondered why such simple advise is so hard to follow. Could it be that we find it so difficult to "be ourselves" because we do not have a clear concept of who we are? If so, Paul's words in Galatians 5:24–25 will prove very helpful. He boils down our essential identity to three crucial elements and then exhorts us to behave accordingly.

> Now those who belong to Christ Jesus have crucified the flesh with its passion and desires. If we live by the Spirit, let us also walk by the Spirit.

Who are we, Christians? According to Paul, we are those who (1) belong to Christ Jesus, (2) have crucified the flesh with its passions and desires, and (3) live by the Spirit. We are not our own (1 Corinthians 6:19–20). God chose us before time began (Ephesians 1:4) to be part of a people He would give to His Son (John 17:6, 9–10, 12). We are the church, the bride of Christ. We are a gift of love God gives to Jesus.

Unlike most gifts, however, we came at great cost to the recipient. We were in bondage to sin—polluted, soiled, and in debt to God. Before Jesus Christ could possess us, He had to redeem us. The bride-price He paid freed us from sin's authority, clothed us in His righteousness, and settled in full our account with God. Jesus identified with us by becoming a man, earned perfect righteousness for us with His perfect life, and paid off our debt. He laid claim to us by promising never to leave or forsake us and sending His Spirit to live in us until He comes back to get us (John 14:16–18).

Jesus Christ's work on our behalf makes us new creations (2 Corinthians 5:17). In the power of His indwelling Spirit, we have crucified the flesh with its passions and desires—executed it in the sense that we live free of its bondage (Romans 6:6). Although the flesh was dealt a death blow by our regeneration, it has not yet succumbed. It has been fatally wounded, but will not breathe its last until we are glorified. We live in a challenging relationship with our dying flesh. We dare not ignore it, but neither should we give in to it. The crucified flesh is clearly a force to be reckoned with, but it is also a force we are *fully able* to reckon with.

We who belong to Christ Jesus live by the Spirit, not by the flesh. The indwelling Spirit gives us new life that unites us with Christ, transforms our desires, and empowers us to walk worthy of our high calling. His divine power has given us everything that we need to pursue practical holiness and escape the corruption of fleshly desire. We are a people belonging to Christ, selected, rebuilt, and redirected to proclaim His excellencies. We resist the flesh because of *who we are*. We are free in Christ, equipped by His Spirit to live for His glory.

*Knowing* who we are equips us to *be* who we are—and to walk by the Spirit.

# *Notes*

1. John MacArthur uses this incident to illustrate a point in his commentary on Galatians (*Galatians*, The MacArthur New Testament Commentary [Chicago: Moody Press, 1987], 97). I did a little research of my own on T. E. Lawrence and wrote my own account of this incident as the introduction to this lesson.

2. See Romans 6.

3. One good example of this comparison is in chapter 15 of Jerry Bridges's outstanding book *The Gospel for Real Life* (Colorado Springs: NavPress, 2002), 179–83.

4. See note 6 following lesson 10.

5. MacArthur, *Galatians*, 162.

6. James Montgomery Boice, *The Expositor's Bible Commentary*, vol. 10, *Romans–Galatians* (Grand Rapids, Mich.: Zondervan, 1976), 497.

7. MacArthur, *Galatians*, 161.

8. Philip Graham Ryken, *Galatians*, Reformed Expository Commentary (Phillipsburg, N.J.: P&R Publishing, 2005), 235.

9. Most reliable commentators admit a bit of uncertainty when discussing the meaning of Paul's statement, "against such things there is no law." But most of their cautious comments converge around the idea that bearing the fruit of the Spirit results from regenerate internal desire rather than legalistic external conformity to the law. Most also emphasize that Christians who are led by the Spirit will obey God's law.

10. Quoted in Ryken, *Galatians*, 236.

# E X E R C I S E S

1. Read Galatians 5:1, 13, 16–25; Romans 6:1–7:13; 1 Peter 2:9–3:18; Ephesians 2:8–10; Matthew 5:16; and Titus 2:11–14. Then use what you learn from these verses to write a description of Christian freedom. Be sure to include the purpose of Christian freedom.

2. In your own words, describe the sure link between justification and sanctification.

3. What does "glorifying God" look like in everyday life? Include a few real-life examples in your response.

4. Are Christians free to disobey God's law? Explain.

5. Describe the inherent differences between those who are controlled by the flesh and those who live by the Spirit. What generates these inherent differences?

6. List each "deed of the flesh" and "fruit of the Spirit," along with a brief definition. How do these two lists help us "test [ourselves] to see if [we] are in the faith" (2 Corinthians 13:5)?

7. How can we most effectively obey Paul's command to walk by the Spirit?

APPLICATION

1. This week review previous memory verses and begin memorizing one or more of the following Scripture passages:

   Ezekiel 11:19–20 or 36:26–27

   Matthew 5:16

   Psalm 1:1–6

2. This week in your prayer time, use Galatians 5:24–25 to help you focus on who you are in Christ. Express your gratitude to God for giving you to Jesus Christ, equipping you to crucify the flesh with its passions and desires, and making you live by the Spirit. Praise God for His perfect plan of salvation, which empowers you to walk worthy of your high calling in Christ. Identify and confess your failures to walk by the Spirit, and seek His help to recognize and act on opportunities to exalt God through your behavior this week.

3. Who are you, Christian? Write a character sketch of yourself based on what you have learned thus far in your study of Galatians. Then list one or more specific ways in which knowing who you are in Christ will help you fulfill your chief end more effectively. (See Application exercise 4 for an explanation of what a "specific" response looks like.)

4. Read each of the following verses. Then describe what each one teaches about where, how, or toward what the Holy Spirit leads you. In your description, include one or more *specific* examples of the Spirit's leading in your life. (Specific examples include specific situations, times, places, people, attitudes, words, and actions. Please do not answer this question with vague generalities. For example, a vague generality would sound something like this: "The Holy Spirit helped me pray more effectively this week by convicting me of some sins." On the other hand, a specific example would sound more like this: "The Holy Spirit helped me understand and apply Philippians 2:14–15 when I was habitually complaining about circumstances

at work last week. He used this verse to convict me of my sins of discontentment, self-centeredness, and laziness—and urged me to confess them to God in prayer and seek forgiveness. He also helped me to see that my primary focus at work should be keeping my behavior before unbelievers 'above reproach' so I can be a more effective light in the world. I am now seeking God's help in prayer as I work on replacing complaining and disputing with thoughts, words, and actions that reflect the love, care, and provision with which God blesses me through my work."):

John 15:26; 16:13–15

Acts 1:8

Romans 7:6–7; John 16:14

Romans 8:15–17

Galatians 5:1, 18

Galatians 5:16–17, 19–21

Galatians 5:22–25; 6:8–10

Ephesians 2:18; Hebrews 4:14–16

Ephesians 5:18–21

## DIGGING DEEPER

Paul's words in Galatians 5:23 ("against *such things* there is no law") indicate that he may not be limiting the fruit of the Spirit to the nine examples he lists in 5:22–23. John W. Sanderson, in *The Fruit of the Spirit* (1972; reprint, Phillipsburg, N.J.: Presbyterian and Reformed, 1985), says that there is "no official checklist" for the fruit of the Spirit (p. 41). He gives four other places in Scripture where "fruit of the Spirit" are found: Romans 5:3–5; 1 Timothy 6:11; 2 Timothy 3:10–11; and 2 Peter 1:5–9. Read these passages with Sanderson's idea in mind. After prayerfully considering these passages, state whether you agree with Sanderson and defend your position from Scripture.

### Primary Passage
GALATIANS 5:26–6:10

### Supplementary Passages
JOB 4:7–11
PSALM 55:22
ISAIAH 40:27–31
HOSEA 8:7
MATTHEW 7:1–5; 11:25–30
JOHN 13:34–35
ROMANS 2:5–11; 8:1–39; 12:3; 13:8–10; 14:10–12; 15:1
1 CORINTHIANS 12:12–14
2 CORINTHIANS 9:6–11; 10:12, 17–18
EPHESIANS 4:31–32
PHILIPPIANS 2:12–13
1 THESSALONIANS 5:14
HEBREWS 12:1–3, 12–13
JAMES 1:22
1 PETER 2:9–10; 5:6–7
1 JOHN 1:5–9

Before reading the lesson material, please read the primary Scripture passage listed above and as many of the supplementary passages as time allows. Then briefly summarize in your notebook what you have read. (Do not go into detail. Limit your summary to a brief description of the people, events, and/or ideas discussed in the passages.)

# Spiritual Rescue

*Be united with other Christians. A wall with loose bricks is not good. The bricks must be cemented together.*
—Corrie ten Boom

———— 🌿 ————

I recently returned from a lovely weekend in Montgomery, Texas, where I met many new friends while speaking at a women's retreat sponsored by Lakeside Bible Church. The church is appropriately named, as is the Del Lago[1] resort area, where I spent Saturday night. Church and hotel sit on opposite sides of a large, beautiful lake—something I rarely see in my native New Mexico.

Something else I rarely see in New Mexico is a little insect known as a mosquito that likes to hang out near large bodies of water. I recognized a few of them loitering on the outside of my patio door Sunday morning but remained blissfully unaware that at least one of the little critters had spent the night in my room.

After a wonderful worship service and fellowship meal at Lakeside, two dear ladies drove me to the airport in Houston. It was not until after I found my departure gate and settled into a chair that I realized my right eye was burning and itching. *Eyestrain*, I told myself and reached for the artificial tears I carry for just such emergencies.

They didn't help much, and by the time I boarded the airplane, I was mildly distressed. Tugging on the outside corner of my eyelid brought some relief, and I spent most of the flight doing just that. Consequently, by the time my husband, Frank, met me in Albuquerque, my poor eye was not only burning and itching but also swollen and red. "Allergies," Frank wisely opined and lovingly suggested that I take a Claritin™.

The next morning I awoke far beyond mildly distressed. My eye was burning and itching so badly I couldn't concentrate on anything else. I struggled through a few errands and chores before finally deciding to visit my eye doctor. After a brief exam, he informed me that I had a mosquito bite on my eyeball. After chuckling that he had never seen such a thing in his thirty-year practice, he prescribed some soothing drops and advised me to watch out for signs of infection. Fortunately, no infection developed and, within a few days, I was back to normal.

Since then, I have not given my odd injury much thought—until this week when I began pondering Galatians 5:26–6:10. In this passage, Paul exhorted the Galatians to forgo self-absorption and help sinful brethren walk by the Spirit rather than by the flesh. He instructed them to patiently correct those caught in sin, to lovingly support those who are vulnerable, and to alertly resist the temptations associated with that kind of ministry. He told those who receive instruction to share all good things with their teachers, advised the Galatians that they would reap what they sow, and then urged them not to grow weary in doing good.

After hours of study, I understood *what* Paul had said. But remembering the mosquito bite on my eyeball helped me "see" *why* he had said it. The puncture wound in my eye was tiny—invisible without the aid of my eye doctor's equipment. And yet it created sufficient distress to sideline my whole body from its normal pursuits. I simply could not ignore it and get on with my other activities. And I did not know how to heal the injury myself. I needed a medically qualified caregiver to come to my rescue.

Paul's beloved, bewitched brethren in the churches of Galatia were in similar circumstances. They had been injured by deceptive false teaching. And Paul knew that the injury could not be ignored. The Galatians were part of the body of Christ, whose spiritual function is impaired when a member is injured. The very nature of the Galatians' injury left them unable to heal it themselves. They needed a spiritually qualified caregiver to come to their rescue.

Like most analogies, this one has limitations. Paul, like my eye doctor, was a qualified caregiver who came to the Galatians' rescue when they could not help themselves. Unlike my eye doctor, however, he went beyond rescue to equipping them to minister to one another without his intervention.

## From Rescued to Rescuers

### (Galatians 5:26–6:5)

Paul came to the Galatians' rescue by writing the letter we are studying. Paul's letter amounts to a four-step rescue operation. And thus far, we have seen him accomplish three of those steps. Think back over our previous lessons and recall how Paul has: (1) affirmed that his apostolic credentials qualify him to come to their rescue; (2) diagnosed the Galatians' condition as acute gullibility under the influence of clever deceivers; and (3) prescribed the sure cure of understanding and living out God's gospel of grace.

Now as Paul nears the end of his letter, he embarks on step four: teaching the Galatians how to deal with future injuries. In Galatians 5:26–6:10, Paul completed his rescue effort by equipping them to do for each other what he had done for them. Paul knew that the best defense against spiritual injury is the good offense of a well-functioning spiritual body. And therefore, he exhorted the Galatians to build strong walls of unity by *helping each other* crucify the flesh with its passions and desires and walk as they lived—by the Spirit.

> Let us not become boastful, challenging one another, envying one another. Brethren, even if anyone is caught in any trespass, you who are spiritual, restore such a one in a spirit of gentleness; each one looking to yourself, so that you too will not be tempted. Bear one another's burdens, and thereby fulfill the law of Christ. For if anyone thinks he is something when he is nothing, he deceives himself. But each one must examine his own work, and then he will have reason for boasting in regard to himself alone, and not in regard to another. For each one will bear his own load. (5:26–6:5)

The first point Paul made was that strong walls of unity are not built by the boastful. That is because boastful people are self-absorbed and self-serving. They walk by the flesh, not by the Spirit, in relationships marked by challenge and envy. They argue contentiously at the drop of a hat and resent those who don't fuel their high regard for themselves. They specialize in disturbance and discord, division and discouragement, disparagement and defamation. And they consistently fail to edify or enlighten, encourage or elevate, equip or enable. They are better at bombarding strong walls of unity than they are at building them—and thus, do not qualify as spiritual rescuers.

Spiritually qualified rescuers are good at maintaining a selfless focus. They know that the church's primary mission is to honor and glorify God. They understand that because the church is a body, fulfilling that mission is a joint effort. And they realize that well-functioning life in the body combines personal responsibility for individual holiness with mutual obligation to support one another in that pursuit.

Strong walls of unity are cemented together when spiritually qualified rescuers rush to the aid of brothers or sisters who are "caught in any trespass." Most commentators understand the phrase translated "caught in any trespass" to mean a moral stumble, a slip into uncharacteristic sinful behavior, or a lack of diligence in resisting assaults from the world, the flesh, and the devil.[2] This is precisely what the Galatians had done. They were not hardened, rebellious, aggressive sinners who gave every evidence of being potential apostates or infiltrating wolves. Paul relegated the deceitful false teachers to that category and responded to them accordingly. The Galatian believers, however, he treated as brethren who had tripped and fallen in their pursuit of holiness—and who were likely to do it again. He exhorted them to learn from his example how to rescue each other.

Those "who are spiritual," he said, must "restore" those who fall "in a spirit of gentleness" and with an attitude of humility. Notice he did not give this assignment to "those who are sinless," or even to "those who are seasoned and mature in their faith."

That is because no Christian is sinless, and even seasoned, mature believers periodically trip and fall in their pursuit of holiness. So who are "the spiritual"? The context strongly suggests that they are those who, at the time a brother or sister needs help, are walking by the Spirit and not by the flesh.

All believers in Jesus Christ are indwelt by God's Spirit and thus inclined and equipped to walk by the Spirit. But because we live "in the flesh," we remain highly vulnerable to fleshly temptations. Believers at all levels of maturity in Christ are snared by these temptations from time to time. And believers at all levels of maturity who are walking by the Spirit at those times are able and responsible to run to their aid.[3]

Restoring those caught in any trespass is a mending process directed at rebuilding strength, resetting focus, and reclaiming usefulness. It necessarily includes some rebuke and correction, which may create stumbling blocks for all parties involved. Those in need of restoration may be tempted to excuse their behavior, respond in anger, or sink into despair. Those attempting to restore may be tempted to feel superior, seek revenge, or yield to the very sin the brother or sister committed.

That is why Paul cautioned the Galatians to restore in a spirit of gentleness and with an attitude of humility. Gentleness is a fruit of the Spirit that defuses antagonism and encourages those who have fallen to confess their sin, repent, seek forgiveness, and return to pursuing holiness in the power of the Spirit for the glory of God. Humility acknowledges vulnerability to the allures of the flesh and encourages those who restore to rely on the Spirit to equip them to minister effectively.

Spiritually qualified rescuers "fulfill the law of Christ" when love for their brethren compels them to "bear one another's burdens." The Greek word translated "burdens" refers to heavy loads that are very difficult to carry alone. It could refer to a trial or temptation of overwhelming intensity or demoralizing persistence. The love that willingly shoulders another's burden flows from deep commitment to the joint effort required to fulfill the church's primary mission of giving God honor and glory.

That kind of love is suppressed when believers deceive themselves into thinking they are something when they are nothing. Regarding themselves as too important or too busy or even too holy to assist a fallen sinner, they ignore injured members—and eventually pay the price. The body of Christ is a living, systemic, unified whole—not a loosely amalgamated collection of self-contained saints. One injured saint inevitably affects all the others.

Paul commanded the Galatians to "examine their own work" and "bear their own load." Each believer in Christ must do his or her part in maintaining the health and strength of Christ's body. We examine our "own work," not by comparing it to what others are doing, but by evaluating it against the standard of what God requires of us. Just as Jesus told Peter, "Follow Me!" without comparing his tasks to John's (John 21:18–23), Paul informed the Galatians that they were responsible to bear their own load.

The Greek word translated "load" refers to something that is intended to be carried alone—like a ship's cargo, a soldier's equipment, or a hiker's backpack. These loads are assembled with the abilities and limitations of the carrier in mind. The measurements of a ship's hold and the strength of a soldier or hiker are carefully considered when their loads are assembled. In much the same way, God "loads" His children according to their gifts, abilities, strengths, and maturity—and expects us to carry what we have been given in the power of His Spirit for the display of His glory.

Although the size and shape of our loads differ, each includes an obligation to help others bear burdens.

## Never Give Up!

### *(Galatians 6:6–10)*

Paul did not give his Galatian brethren the option of becoming spiritually qualified rescuers. He did not suggest that they might pursue this ministry opportunity if they felt so inclined. Nor did he assure them that he would understand fully if they just weren't up to it right now.

In Galatians 6:1–5, Paul depicted spiritual rescue as a necessary joint effort involving all members of the body of Christ and commanded the Galatians to *help one another* walk by the Spirit instead of the flesh. But he did not stop there. Paul knew he was calling his brethren to difficult ministry. And he knew that those who rose to the challenge would often be tempted to give up in frustration. So he went on to *encourage* his Galatian brethren to persevere in the task of spiritual rescue. In Galatians 6:6–10, Paul urges them to focus on building Christ-honoring fellowship while relying completely on the equipping power of the indwelling Spirit.

> The one who is taught the word is to share all good things with the one who teaches him. Do not be deceived, God is not mocked; for whatever a man sows, this he will also reap. For the one who sows to his own flesh will from the flesh reap corruption, but the one who sows to the Spirit will from the Spirit reap eternal life. Let us not lose heart in doing good, for in due time we will reap if we do not grow weary. So then, while we have opportunity, let us do good to all people, and especially to those who are of the household of the faith.

Most commentators understand Galatians 6:6 as a mandate to provide material support for pastor-teachers so that they will have time and energy to minister most effectively to their congregations. However, a few take an intriguingly different view. They assert that Paul was, in fact, describing the restoration of Christ-honoring fellowship that results from restoring those caught in any trespass.

In my opinion, they support their assertion with three very good points. First, they indicate that the idea of material support is out of context with the rest of the passage. Second, they acknowledge that verse 6 could accurately be translated, "Let him who is taught share (or fellowship) with him who teaches *in* all good things." And finally, they point out that Paul used the same word (translated "good things" and "good") in verses 6 and 10—a word that refers primarily to spiritual and moral excellence rather than material good. (The same word is also used in Romans 10:15 and Hebrews 9:11.)[4]

If the minority opinion is right in this case (and I am inclined to think that it is), the "good things" being shared in verse 6 are spiritual, not material. Advocates of this view conclude that Paul was not championing a paid pastorate here (although he certainly did elsewhere). Rather, he was describing the way those caught in any trespass are restored to useful fellowship in the body of Christ when they respond rightly to God's Word as it is taught by those who are spiritual.[5]

The ministry of restoration clearly enhances the church's ability to pursue its primary mission of giving God honor and glory. However, this essential ministry is rarely easy. That is because, even though all parties involved are in union with Christ and indwelt by His Spirit, they also live "in the flesh" and are susceptible to its allure. Thus, those "caught in any trespass" are inclined to resist rebuke and correction. And those "who are spiritual" eventually tend to give up in frustration.

Paul affirmed that the success of spiritual rescue depends on the submission of all parties involved to the indwelling Spirit. The irrefutable agricultural principle of sowing and reaping applies just as inexorably to the process of restoring Christ-honoring fellowship as it does to growing corn, beans, or wheat. Farmers do not harvest beans by planting corn seeds. And Christians do not sharpen the reflection and deepen the enjoyment of the eternal life we have been given when we either minister in the flesh or respond that way to the ministry efforts of others. Only as we rely on the Spirit's empowering as we participate in the ministry of restoration will we contribute significantly to the fulfillment of the church's primary mission.

When I was in college and struggling with a particularly difficult class, a friend encouraged me greatly by slipping a cartoon into my textbook. It pictured a large bird of some sort that had swallowed about one-third of a frog. The remaining two-thirds of the frog hung outside of the bird's beak, and the frog's "hands" were wrapped tightly around the bird's neck. The cartoon's caption read, "Never give up!"

Paul encouraged the Galatians in much the same way when he said, "Let us not lose heart in doing good, for in due time we will reap if we do not grow weary." Paul was well-acquainted with the temptation to grow weary in doing good. His ministry had subjected him to great physical distress as well as the crushing emotional burden of "concern for all churches" (2 Corinthians 11:23–28). And we have seen ample evidence in this study that his ministry to the Galatians had been especially difficult.

But Paul knew (for a fact without any doubt) that Spirit-empowered ministry yields Spirit-inspired results. He was confident that his difficult ministry among the Galatians would bear fruit. And he was equally confident that as they relied on the Spirit's power to minister to each other the way he had ministered to them, "the whole body, being fitted and held together by what every joint supplies, according to the proper working of each individual part," would stimulate "the growth of the body for the building up of itself in love" (Ephesians 4:16).

Thus, he urged them to join in following his example by viewing life on this earth as an extended "opportunity" to "do [spiritual] good to all people, and especially to those who are of the household of faith."

## Notes

1. *Del Lago* is Spanish for "of the lake."

2. Most of these commentators point out that although the word translated "caught" could mean "discovered," the primary idea is not that the sinner has been "exposed" but that he or she has been "snared."

3. The Holy Spirit always works with God's Word. (In Ephesians 5:15–6:9 and Colossians 3:16–4:6, Paul equates "being filled with the Spirit" with "letting the Word dwell in you richly" by demonstrating that the same results flow from each.) Obviously, walking by the Spirit does not occur in a vacuum. Those who effectively walk by the Spirit are those who understand God's truth and wisely apply it to situations of life.

4. Of the few commentators I read who hold this minority view, John MacArthur seems to do the best job of defending it (to my mind, at least). See *Galatians*, The MacArthur

New Testament Commentary (Chicago: Moody Press, 1987), 182.

5. The interpretation of Galatians 6:6 is *not* one of those hills upon which I am willing to die. However, this minority interpretation seems to me to best fit Paul's flow of thought.

## E x e r c i s e s

### Review

1. How does Paul's letter to the Galatians resemble a rescue operation? Why did the Galatians need rescuing? Why was Paul so committed to rescuing them?

2. What is the best defense against spiritual injury? How do Christians go about building this defense?

3. What disqualifies the boastful from being spiritual rescuers?

4. What does the phrase "caught in any trespass" mean?

5. Who are "the spiritual" to whom Paul refers in Galatians 6:1? How does the context of Galatians 6:1 help you identify whom he had in mind when he used this term?

6. In your own words, describe how the process of restoration should be carried out.

7. Describe the difference between bearing one another's burdens and carrying your own load. How do both contribute to the health and vitality of the body of Christ?

8. How do those commentators who believe Paul is *not* championing a paid pastorate in Galatians 6:6 support their view?

9. How does the ministry of restoration enhance the church's ability to pursue its primary mission of giving God honor and glory? What makes this ministry difficult?

10. How does the irrefutable agricultural principle of sowing and reaping apply to the ministry of restoration?

## APPLICATION

1. This week review previous memory verses and begin memorizing one or more of the following Scripture passages:

   John 13:34–35
   Galatians 6:9–10
   Ephesians 4:31–32

2. This week in your prayer time, review Paul's letter to the Galatians, focusing on the way he exemplified the ministry of restoration. Thank God for Paul's example in this letter and ask God to help you learn from Paul how to participate in this ministry more effectively.

3. American Christians live in a culture that elevates self-esteem above esteeming others, values self-sufficiency higher than interdependence, extols self-indulgence rather than self-restraint, encourages self-promotion over self-sacrifice, and prizes celebrity more than humility. Even though we have been redeemed by God's Son and transformed by His Spirit, we are not immune to cultural influences. The plague of self-centered individualism infecting our nation constantly tempts us to walk by the flesh instead of the Spirit. Prayerfully evaluate your own tendencies to submit to your culture instead of your Lord. Identify and list several specific areas in which you are particularly vulnerable to self-centered temptations of the flesh. How do these weaknesses hinder your

participation in the ministry of spiritual rescue? Seek counsel from your pastor, another of your church leaders, or a mature Christian friend or relative concerning how you might begin strengthening your areas of weakness so that you will be more effective in building Christ-honoring fellowship within your church family.

4. In Galatians 6:10, Paul does not identify specific ways in which we should "do good to all people, and especially to those who are of the household of the faith." So let's expand on his statement by asking ourselves a few pertinent questions: Am I eager to do good for all people, and do I look for creative ways to do so? (If not, confess your sin of self-centeredness and seek the Holy Spirit's help to turn from it.) Who are several people (list them by name) for whom I can do something good? Do I have believers and unbelievers on my list? (If not, revise your list.) What specific good things can I do for these people? (List specific actions beside each name.) When and where will I do these good things? (List specific times and places.) How will I do these good things? (Include both methodology and attitude.) Does your list of good things include both material good things and spiritual good things? (If not, revise your list.) Does it include any restoration activities? (If not, should it?) Share your list with someone who loves you enough to hold you accountable to follow through on your plans and who also loves you enough to encourage you not to grow weary in doing good.

## DIGGING DEEPER

Those who make a good living in real estate usually adhere to the axiom, "Location! Location! Location!" And those who consistently interpret Scripture well usually subscribe to the corresponding principle of "Context! Context! Context!" Study Galatians 6:6 in context. Include in your study an investigation of how those who hold differing views regarding the meaning of this passage support their views. Seek input from your pastor, other church leaders, or Bible teachers. Then determine which view seems to best fit the flow of Paul's thought in Galatians 5:26–6:10. Is context alone sufficient to determine the meaning of the verse? What other factors should be considered? (If you are unfamiliar with effective Bible study methods, consult my book *Turning On the Light* and any of the other books included in the "Recommended Reading" section of that book.)

*Primary Passage*
GALATIANS 6:11–18

*Supplementary Passages*
ISAIAH 29:13–14
EZEKIEL 33:1–9
MATTHEW 6:1–18; 23:1–33
LUKE 16:14–15; 18:9–14
ACTS 5:17–42
ROMANS 2:25–29; 3:27–30; 6:15–23
1 CORINTHIANS 1:17–31; 10:31
2 CORINTHIANS 5:17–21; 10:17–18; 11:23–28; 12:7–10
PHILIPPIANS 1:29–30; 3:7–14, 18–21
COLOSSIANS 2:8
2 TIMOTHY 3:1–5.

Before reading the lesson material, please read the primary
Scripture passage listed above and as many of the supplementary passages as time allows. Then briefly summarize in
your notebook what you have read. (Do not go into detail.
Limit your summary to a brief description of the people,
events, and/or ideas discussed in the passages.)

# Distinguish and Stand

*Make us choose the harder right instead of the easier wrong,
and never to be contented with half truth when whole truth
can be won.* —FROM THE UNITED STATES MILITARY
ACADEMY'S "CADET PRAYER"

It was a dramatic moment. The renegade monk gripped the
edge of the table separating him from his inquisitors and
gazed at the pile of books it supported. The Archbishop's question rang in his ears, "Brother Martin. Are these your books?"
Luther's stomach knotted. He had no doubt where his answer
would lead. "They are all mine," he said quietly. "And I have
written more."

"Do you defend them all, or do you care to reject a part?"

After pausing to ponder this momentous question, Brother Martin surprised everyone present by requesting time to think it over. Permission was granted, and he retired to a sleepless night of earnestly seeking God's guidance in prayer. The next day he returned to the council and mounted an heroic defense of his work ending with these now-famous words:

> Since your Majesty and your lordships desire a simple reply, I will answer without horns and without teeth. Unless I am convinced by Scripture and plain reason—I do not accept the authority of popes and councils, for they have contradicted each other—my conscience is captive to the Word of God. I cannot and will not recant anything, for to go against conscience is neither right nor safe. God help me. Here I stand, I cannot do otherwise. Amen.[1]

Long before the United States Military Academy's "Cadet Prayer" was written, Martin Luther chose the harder right over the easier wrong and refused to be contented with half-truth when full truth could be won. And long before Luther made this well-considered bold stand, Paul closed his letter to the Galatians by challenging his beloved, bewitched brethren to do the same thing.

In Galatians 6:11–18, Paul crystallized the distinction between the Judaizers' easier wrong of flesh-centered false doctrine and the harder right of his Christ-centered gospel. Then he called his Galatian brethren to reject the half-truths of works-righteousness and stand firm in the full truth of God's revelation.

## A Clear Distinction

### *(Galatians 6:11–15)*

Paul knew there are only two kinds of religion: Christianity and everything else. Christianity is the religion of divine accomplishment. It is grounded in God's grace, received by God-given faith, and lived out in the power of God's Holy Spirit. Everything else is the religion of human achievement. Every religion besides Christianity is grounded in rule-keeping, received by works-righteousness, and lived out in the flesh.

Paul had taught the Galatians the unique truth of God, but smooth-talking false teachers later blurred the distinction between Christianity and everything else. They preached a hybrid gospel of faith plus works-righteousness, which Paul recognized as dangerously pseudo-Christian. Distressed to learn that his beloved brethren had failed to distinguish between truth and error, Paul wrote with an urgency that approached severity to clarify the distinction between Christianity and everything else.

In our study so far, we have seen Paul effectively counter the Judaizers' three primary assaults against Christianity's essence: apostolic authority, justification, and sanctification. Paul began by establishing his apostolic authority to speak truth from God—thereby indicating that those who disagreed with his doctrine were necessarily disagreeing with God. Next, he affirmed that right standing with God comes only by grace alone through faith alone in Christ alone—thereby denying that works-righteousness plays any part in redemption. And finally, Paul declared that the indwelling Spirit unites us with Christ, gives us a new nature, and frees us to pursue holiness in the power of the Spirit for the glory of God—thereby asserting that Christian living is neither fueled by the flesh nor meant to be self-exalting.

Paul's arguments not only distinguished true from false doctrine. They also contrasted his true shepherd's heart with the wolfish motives characterizing the Judaizers. Paul's rescue effort was prompted by an intense love and concern for the eternal welfare of foolishly credulous saints, whereas the Judaizers were driven by self-serving agendas.

As we look now at Paul's concluding remarks, we will first focus on his summary distinction between his appeal to the Galatians and that of the Judaizers.

> See with what large letters I am writing to you with my own hand. Those who desire to make a good showing in the flesh try to compel you to be circumcised, simply so that they will not be persecuted for the cross of Christ. For those who are circumcised do not even keep the Law themselves, but they desire to have you circumcised so that they may boast in your flesh. But may it never be that I would boast, except in the cross of our Lord Jesus Christ, through which the world has been crucified to me, and I to the world. For neither is circumcision anything, nor uncircumcision, but a new creation. (6:11–15)

If the apostle Paul had had access to a laptop computer complete with the latest word-processing software, he no doubt would have sprinkled his concluding remarks to the Galatians with **bold**, *italicized **words and phrases*** instead of "large letters" in his "own hand." Most commentators[2] suggest that he used the most effective writing technique available to emphasize the essential distinction between true and false teachers: whether or not their "boasting" reflects "a new creation."

God's gospel of grace is about new creation. It is about God's redeeming and transforming sinners, against their own merit, through the work of His Son Jesus Christ. It is about those who have been tried, convicted, and sentenced to death receiving the indescribable free gift of new life and new purpose. It is about crucifixion and resurrection, dying to self and living "in Christ," spurning works-righteousness and claiming Christ's righteousness. It is about what God did for us, not what we do for Him.

The essential distinction between true and false teachers, Paul said, is that the true boast in God's work, whereas the false boast in their own. The boast of true teachers reflects their transformation in Christ—the "new creation" they are because of what God has done in them through the work of His Son. The boast of false teachers reflects their self-absorbed fallenness—the fleshly creatures they are because of what they do for themselves through their own efforts.

Paul drew that distinction so sharply because he cared so deeply for the spiritual welfare of his Galatian brethren. In keeping with his passionate pursuit of God's best for them, he concluded by challenging them to replace gullibility with wise discernment. "Allow me to summarize your situation," he said in effect. "The Judaizers don't have your best interests at heart. They are primarily concerned with their own prestige and safety. They add circumcision to faith in Christ Jesus because it appeases the Jews. The Judaizers don't want to be persecuted by Jews who despise the gracious implications of Christ's death on the cross. So even though they don't keep the law themselves, they compel you to be circumcised and then boast in the number of you who comply.

"I, on the other hand," Paul continued, "want nothing more than to boast in the cross of our Lord Jesus Christ. I know I cannot merit right standing with God. Indeed, I know I have merited nothing but wrath. But I have been given an indescribable gift, which I cherish above anything in this world. I have received justification because Jesus Christ took my place on the cross and atoned for my sin. His work on the cross redeemed me from bondage to the world, the flesh, and the devil. I am united with Him; His Spirit lives in me. My desires and abilities have been transformed for the purpose of pursuing Christlikeness. His work on the cross resulted in the world being crucified to me and me to the world. The things I once counted as gain, I now count as rubbish. Those who once regarded me with esteem, now look at me with contempt. But I have lost nothing of value. Knowing and serving my Lord Jesus Christ far surpasses whatever this world has to offer."

*"Can you discern the difference between the Judaizers and me?"* Paul, in effect, emphatically challenged his readers. *"Do you see that circumcision is downright irrelevant? Do you see that the state of your flesh is of no interest to God? Do you see that He is concerned with the state of your soul? Do you see that what matters is a new creation?"*

## Stand Firm on Full Truth

### (Galatians 6:16–18)

At this point, I picture Paul sighing deeply, laying his pen on the table, and pausing to pray for his beloved brethren in the regions of Galatia. He had said everything God had laid on his heart—written urgently with deep pastoral concern in a no-holds-barred effort to turn them from error. What more could he say? Only that the ball was in their court. The options were clear and the choice was theirs. Would they choose the harder right of his Christ-centered gospel or the easier wrong of flesh-centered false doctrine?

I imagine Paul finally lifting his head, sighing deeply again, and re-gripping his pen. Hastily scrawling three final sentences, I see him seal the letter decisively and call for the messenger.

> And those who will walk by this rule, peace and mercy be upon them, and upon the Israel of God. From now on let no one cause trouble for me, for I bear on my body the brand-marks of Jesus. The grace of our Lord Jesus Christ be with your spirit, brethren. Amen. (6:16–18)

The seriousness of the situation in Galatia is as evident at the end of Paul's letter as it was at the beginning. Just as his salutation included no warm words of praise or thanksgiving for them, his closing contained no friendly greetings or news of the brethren. Instead it consisted of three terse, simple sentences comprising one last urgent appeal. There was, in reality, only one right course of action. Paul hoped they would hear him with understanding and follow his example of standing firm on full truth. With every ounce of his being, he wanted the Galatians to know and reflect the incomparable glory of God's gospel of grace.

Peace and mercy, Paul said, are for those who choose to "walk by this rule." In other words, the serenity of heart and mind that results from receiving God's loving-kindness toward sinners is only for those who hope in the cross. It is only for those who have counted all things of this world to be rubbish because of the surpassing value of knowing Christ Jesus as Lord. It is only for the "Israel of God"—true Israel, Abraham's spiritual descendants, whose faith has been credited to them as righteousness. It is only for those who choose to stand firm on the full truth of God.

Paul urged the Galatians to choose the harder right over the easier wrong. He pled with them not to be contented with half-truth when full truth could be had. He knew that they knew what God required of them and what he (Paul) wanted for them. He hoped they would give him no more trouble and follow him as he followed Christ. The "brand-marks" he bore on his body demonstrated true faith—something the mark of circumcision could never do. The "brand-marks of Jesus" signified his commitment to endure all things for the sake of those who are chosen. The mark of circumcision extolled by the Judaizers signified empty ceremonialism at best and self-centered cowardice at worst.

Paul's deepest desire for his Galatian brethren was that they know the unparalleled riches of God's glorious grace. He wanted them to be saved by it, live in it, and proclaim it. He wanted God's grace to be the source of their hope, the strength of their stand, and the well of their joy. He wanted God's grace to redeem them from sin and equip them for service. He wanted God's grace to transform his bewitched brethren into a people for God's own possession who would glorify and enjoy Him forever.

That is why Paul wrote the epistle to the Galatians. And that is why we have studied it. May what we have learned from this study incline and equip us to live for His glory.

### Notes

1. Adapted from the account of this incident in Martin Luther's life in Roland H. Bainton, *Here I Stand: A Life of Martin Luther* (Nashville: Abington, 1950), 141–44.

2. A few commentators believe Paul's "large letters" were the result of poor eyesight or some other physical affliction that made writing particularly difficult for him. Since I lean toward thinking that Paul wrote the whole letter himself, not just the conclusion, I am inclined to agree with those commentators who see Paul's large letters as a means of emphasis.

## Exercises

<u>REVIEW</u>

1. Describe the only two kinds of religion.
2. Summarize how Paul's arguments in the book of Galatians distinguish between true and false doctrine in the areas of apostolic authority, justification, and sanctification.
3. How does Paul summarize the essential distinction between true and false teachers?
4. Describe what Paul meant when he used the phrase, "a new creation."
5. Describe several ways in which Paul boasted in the cross of our Lord Jesus Christ. (You may use examples from Galatians or from any of his other letters with which you are familiar.)
6. Explain what Paul meant when he said, "The world has been crucified to me, and I to the world." Are you able to identify with him in this statement. If so, explain.
7. From Paul's final three sentences, explain what he hoped the Galatians would do now that the ball was in their court.
8. Think and discuss (optional): I am very confident that few, if any, of you read the excerpt from the United States Military Academy's "Cadet Prayer" and thought, "Oh,

they got it wrong. It should read 'easier right' and 'harder wrong'—and being content with half-truth is just fine." Reflect on why you *did not* think that, and then discuss why we humans seem to find doing right harder than doing wrong and to prefer settling for half-truth even when full truth is available.

## APPLICATION

1. Review all the Scripture passages you memorized during this study. Continue to review them on a regular basis for several months or until they are firmly fixed in your mind.

2. In your prayer time this week, use 2 Corinthians 5:17; Galatians 6:17; and Philippians 3:7–14 to help you thank God for making you a new creation, and to seek His guidance and strength to live consistently with who you are in Christ.

3. Describe specifically one or more ways in which your study of Galatians has either clarified or changed your understanding of justification. Describe specifically one or more ways in which your study of Galatians has either clarified or changed your understanding of sanctification. Describe specifically one or more ways in which your daily conduct (thoughts, actions, and attitudes) have changed (or should change) because of your study of Galatians.

## DIGGING DEEPER

Reread the book of Galatians slowly and thoughtfully while carefully reviewing what you have learned in the study about Paul's purpose for writing this letter and the means he employed to accomplish his purpose. Write a purpose statement for the book of Galatians and then reduce your purpose statement to a four- to six-word "title" for the book. Consider the means Paul employed to accomplish his purpose for writing in terms of various themes that are discussed in the letter. Write short, concise theme statements for each major theme in the letter. Then outline the book of Galatians according to these themes. (If you need help with this exercise, consult pp. 39–42 of my book *Turning On the Light: Discovering the Riches of God's Word.*)

# What Must I Do to Be Saved?

A strange sound drifted through the Philippian jail as midnight approached. The sound of human voices—but not the expected groans of the two men who had earlier been beaten with rods and fastened in stocks. Rather, the peaceful singing of praises to their God.

While the other prisoners quietly listened to them, the jailer dozed off, content with the bizarre calm generated by these two preachers, who, hours before, had stirred so much commotion in the city.

Suddenly a deafening roar filled the prison as the ground began to shake violently. Sturdy doors convulsed and popped open. Chains snapped and fell at prisoners' feet. Startled into full wakefulness, the jailer stared, horrified, at the wide-open doors that guaranteed his prisoners' escape—and his death. Under Roman law, jailers paid with their lives when prisoners escaped. Resolutely, he drew his sword, thinking it better to die by his own hand than by Roman execution.

"Stop! Don't harm yourself—we are all here!" a voice boomed from the darkened inner cell. The jailer called for lights and was astonished to discover his prisoners standing quietly amid their broken chains. Trembling with fear, he rushed in and fell at the feet of the two preachers. As soon as he was able, he led them out of the ruined prison and asked in utter astonishment, "Sirs, what must I do to be saved?"

I n the entire history of the world, no one has ever asked a more important question. The jailer's words that day may well have been motivated by his critical physical need, but the response of Paul and Silas addressed his even more critical spiritual need: "Believe in the Lord Jesus, and you shall be saved, you and your household" (Acts 16:31).[1]

If you have never "believed in the Lord Jesus," your spiritual need, just like the jailer's, is critical. As long as your life is stained with sin, God cannot receive you into His presence. The Bible says that sin has placed a separation between you and God (Isaiah 59:2). It goes on to say that your nature has been so permeated by sin that you no longer have any desire to serve and obey God (Romans 3:10–12); therefore, you are not likely to recognize or care that a separation exists. Your situation is truly desperate because those who are separated from God will spend eternity in hell.

Since your sinful nature is unresponsive to God, the only way you can be saved from your desperate situation is for God to take the initiative. And this He has done! Even though all men and women deserve the punishment of hell because of their sin, God's love has prompted Him to save some who will serve Him in obedience. He did this by sending His Son, the Lord Jesus Christ, to remove the barrier of sin between God and His chosen ones (Colossians 2:13–14).

What is there about Jesus that enables Him to do this? First of all, He is God. While He was on earth He said, "He who has seen Me has seen the Father" (John 14:9), and "I and the Father are one" (John 10:30). Because He said these things, you must conclude one of three things about His true identity: He was a lunatic who believed He was God when He wasn't; He was a liar who was willing to die a hideous death for what He knew was a lie; or His words are true and He is God.

Lunatics don't live the way Jesus did, and liars don't die the way He did, so if the Bible's account of Jesus' life and words is true, you can be sure He *is* God.

Since Jesus is God, He is perfectly righteous and holy. God's perfect righteousness and holiness demand that sin be punished (Ezekiel 18:4), and Jesus' perfect righteousness and holiness qualified Him to bear the punishment for the sins of those who will be saved (Romans 6:23). Jesus is the only person who never committed a sin; therefore, the punishment He bore when He died on the cross could be accepted by God as satisfaction of His justice in regard to the sins of others.

If someone you love commits a crime and is sentenced to die, you may offer to die in his place. However, if you have also committed crimes worthy of death, your death cannot satisfy the

213

law's demands for your crimes *and* your loved one's. You can die in his place only if you are innocent of any wrongdoing.

Since Jesus lived a perfect life, God's justice could be satisfied by allowing Him to die for the sins of those who will be saved. Because God is perfectly righteous and holy, He could not act in love at the expense of justice. By sending Jesus to die, God demonstrated His love by acting to satisfy His own justice (Romans 3:26).

Jesus did more than die, however. He also rose from the dead. By raising Jesus from the dead, God declared that He had accepted Jesus' death in the place of those who will be saved. Because Jesus lives eternally with God, those for whom Jesus died can be assured they will also spend eternity in heaven (John 14:1–3). The separation of sin has been removed!

Ah, but the all-important question remains unanswered: What must you do to be saved? If God has sent His Son into the world for sinners, and Jesus Christ died in their place, what is left for you to do? You must respond in faith to what God has done. This is what Paul meant when he told the jailer, "Believe in the Lord Jesus, and you shall be saved."

Believing in the Lord Jesus demands three responses from you: an understanding of the facts regarding your hopeless sinful condition and God's action to remove the sin barrier that separates you from Him; acceptance of those facts as true and applicable to you; and a willingness to trust and depend upon God to save you from sin. This involves willingly placing yourself under His authority and acknowledging His sovereign right to rule over you.

But, you say, how can I do this if sin has eliminated my ability to know and appreciate God's work on my behalf? Rest assured that if you desire to have the sin barrier that separates you from God removed, He is already working to change your natural inability to respond. He is extending His gracious offer of salvation to you and will give you the faith to receive it.

If you believe God is working to call you to Himself, read the words He has written to you in the Bible (begin with the book of John in the New Testament) and pray that His Holy Spirit will help you understand what is written there. Continue to read and pray until you are ready to repent, that is, to turn away from sin and commit yourself to serving God.

Is there any other way you can be saved? God Himself says no, there is not. The Bible He wrote says that Jesus is the only way the sin barrier between you and God can be removed (John 14:6; Acts 4:12). He is your hope, and He is your *only* hope.

If you have questions or need any help in this matter, please write to Carol Ruvolo at cruvolo@aol.com before the day is over. God has said in His Bible that a day of judgment is coming, and after that day no one will be saved (Acts 17:30–31; 2 Thessalonians 1:7–9). The time to act is now.

## Note

1.  For a full biblical account of this event, see Acts 16:11–40.

# What Is the Reformed Faith?

The Reformed faith"[1] can be defined as a theology that describes and explains the sovereign God's revelation of His actions in history to glorify Himself by redeeming selected men and women from the just consequences of their self-inflicted depravity.

It is first and foremost theology (the study of God), not anthropology (the study of man). Reformed thinking concentrates on developing a true knowledge of God that serves as the necessary context for all other knowledge. It affirms that the created world, including humanity, cannot be accurately understood apart from its relationship with the Creator.

The Reformed faith describes and explains God's revelation of Himself and His actions to humanity; it does not consist of people's attempts to define God as they wish. The Reformed faith asserts that God has revealed Himself in two distinct ways.

He reveals His existence, wisdom, and power through the created universe—a process known as natural revelation (Romans 1:18–32); and He reveals His requirements and plans for humankind through His written Word, the Bible—a process known as special revelation (2 Timothy 3:16–17).

Reformed theologians uphold the Bible as the inspired, infallible, inerrant, authoritative, and fully sufficient communication of truth from God to us. When they say the Bible is "inspired," they mean that the Bible was written by God through the agency of human authorship in a miraculous way that preserved the thoughts of God from the taint of human sinfulness (2 Peter 1:20–21).

When they say the Bible is infallible, they mean it is incapable of error, and when they say it is inerrant, they mean the Bible, in actual fact, contains no errors. The Bible is authoritative because it comes from God, whose authority over His creation is absolute (Isaiah 46:9–10). And it is completely sufficient because it contains everything necessary for us to know and live according to God's requirements (2 Peter 1:3–4).

By studying God's revelation of Himself and His work, Reformed theologians have learned two foundational truths that structure their thinking about God's relationship with human beings: God is absolutely sovereign, and people are totally depraved.[2]

Reformed thought affirms that God, by definition, is absolutely sovereign—that is, He controls and superintends every circumstance of life either by direct miraculous intervention or by the ordinary outworking of His providence. Reformed theologians understand that a god who is not sovereign cannot be God, because His power would not be absolute. Since the Reformed faith accepts the Bible's teaching regarding the sovereignty of God, it denies that *anything* occurs outside of God's control.

The Reformed faith affirms the biblical teaching that Adam was created with the ability to sin and chose to do so by disobeying a clear command of God (Genesis 3:1–7). Choosing to sin changed basic human nature and left us unable not to sin—or totally depraved. Total depravity does not mean that all people are as bad as they possibly could be but that every facet of their character is tainted with sin, leaving them incapable and undesirous of fellowship with God. The Reformed faith denies that totally depraved men and women have any ability to seek after or submit to God of their own free will. Left to themselves, totally depraved men and women will remain out of fellowship with God for all eternity.

The only way for any of these men and women to have their fellowship with God restored is for God to take the initiative. And the Bible declares that He has graciously chosen to do so (John 14:16). For His own glory, He has chosen some of those depraved men and women to live in fellowship with Him. His choice is determined by His own good pleasure and not by any virtue in the ones He has chosen. For this reason, grace is defined in Reformed thought as "unmerited favor."

God accomplished the salvation of His chosen ones by sending His Son, the Lord Jesus Christ, to bear God's righteous wrath against sin so that He could forgive those He had chosen. Even though Christ's work was perfect and complete, its intended effectiveness is limited to those who are chosen by God for salvation. Christ would not have been required to suffer any more or any less had a different number been chosen for redemption, but the benefit of His suffering is applied only to those who are called by God to believe in Him.

All of those who are thus effectually called by God will eventually believe and be saved, even though they may resist for a time (John 6:37). They cannot forfeit the salvation they have received (John 10:27–30; Romans 8:31–39).

Reformed thought affirms the clear teaching of the Bible that salvation is by faith alone through Christ alone (John 14:6; Acts 4:12; Ephesians 2:8–9) and that human works play no part in salvation, although they are generated by it (Ephesians 2:10). Salvation transforms a person's nature, giving him or her the ability and the desire to serve and obey God. The unresponsive heart of stone is changed into a sensitive heart of flesh that responds readily to God's voice (Ezekiel 36:25–27) and desires to glorify Him out of gratitude for the indescribable gift of salvation.

Reformed thought affirms that God works in history to redeem His chosen ones through a series of covenants. These covenants define His law, assess penalties for breaking His law, and provide for the imputation of Jesus' vicarious fulfillment of God's requirements to those God intends to redeem.[3]

The Reformed faith affirms that we were created and exist solely to glorify God and denies that God exists to serve us. It affirms that God acts to glorify Himself by putting His attributes on display and that His self-glorifying actions are thoroughly righteous since He is the only Being in creation worthy of glorification. It denies that God is primarily motivated to act by man's needs but affirms that all of God's actions are motivated primarily for His own glory.

The Reformed faith emerged as a distinct belief system during the sixteenth and seventeenth centuries when men like Luther, Calvin, Zwingli, and Knox fought to correct abuses and distortions of Christianity that were rampant in the established Roman church and to restore the purity of the gospel and church life taught by the apostles in the New Testament. Reformed thinkers since their day have sought to align their understanding of God and His actions in history as closely as possible to His truth revealed in the Bible.

## Notes

1. This brief overview of basic Reformed beliefs is not intended to be a full explanation of or apologetic for the Reformed faith. For a more detailed description and analysis of the Reformed faith, see R. C. Sproul, *Grace Unknown* (Grand Rapids, Mich.: Baker, 1997); Loraine Boettner, *The Reformed Faith* (Phillipsburg, N.J.: Presbyterian and Reformed, 1983); *Back to Basics: Rediscovering the Richness of the Reformed Faith*, ed. David G. Hagopian (Phillipsburg, N.J.: P&R Publishing, 1996); William Edgar, *Truth in All Its Glory: Commending the Reformed Faith* (Phillipsburg, N.J.: P&R Publishing, 2004); The Westminster Confession of Faith (with its accompanying catechisms); or the theological writings of John Calvin, B. B. Warfield, Charles Hodge, and Louis Berkhof.

2. Both of these truths are taught throughout the pages of Scripture; however, the sovereignty of God can be seen very clearly in Isaiah 40–60 and in Job 38–42, while the total depravity of man is described quite graphically in Romans 3:10–18.

3. An excellent discussion of these covenants is contained in chapter 5 of Sproul, *Grace Unknown*.

# Recommended Reading

Bridges, Jerry. *The Discipline of Grace: God's Role and Our Role in the Pursuit of Holiness*. Colorado Springs: NavPress, 1994.

———. *The Gospel for Real Life*. Colorado Springs: NavPress, 2002.

———. *Transforming Grace: Living Confidently in God's Unfailing Love*. Colorado Springs: NavPress, 1991.

Brown, Steve. *A Scandalous Freedom: The Radical Nature of the Gospel*. West Monroe, La.: Howard, 2004.

Buchanan, James. *The Doctrine of Justification: An Outline of Its History in the Church and of Its Exposition from Scripture*. 1867. Reprint. Carlisle, Pa.: Banner of Truth, 1961.

Chapell, Bryan. *Holiness by Grace: Delighting in the Joy That Is Our Strength*. Wheaton, Ill.: Crossway, 2001.

Ferguson, Sinclair B. *The Christian Life: A Doctrinal Introduction*. Carlisle, Pa.: Banner of Truth, 1981.

———. *The Holy Spirit*. Contours of Christian Theology. Downers Grove, Ill.: InterVarsity, 1996.

Hoekema, Anthony A. *Saved by Grace*. Grand Rapids, Mich.: Eerdmans, 1989.

Luther, Martin. *The Bondage of the Will: The Master Work of the Great Reformer*. Translated by James I. Packer and O. R. Johnson. Old Tappan, N.J.: Revell, 1957.

MacArthur, John. *Nothing but the Truth: Upholding the Gospel in a Doubting Age*. Wheaton, Ill.: Crossway, 1999.

————. *Why One Way? Defending an Exclusive Claim in an Inclusive World*. Nashville: W, 2002.

Mahaney, C. J. *The Cross-Centered Life: Keeping the Gospel the Main Thing*. Sisters, Ore.: Multnomah, 2002.

Morison, Frank. *Who Moved the Stone?* Downers Grove, Ill.: InterVarsity, n.d.

Murray, John. *Principles of Conduct: Aspects of Biblical Ethics*. Grand Rapids, Mich.: Eerdmans, 1957 (particularly chaps. 8–10).

Packer, J. I. *Knowing God*. Twentieth-anniversary edition. Downers Grove, Ill.: InterVarsity, 1993.

Pearcey, Nancy. *Total Truth: Liberating Christianity from Its Cultural Captivity*. Wheaton, Ill.: Crossway, 2004.

Piper, John. *Counted Righteous in Christ: Should We Abandon the Imputation of Christ's Righteousness?* Wheaton, Ill.: Crossway, 2002.

Ryken, Philip G. *The Message of Salvation: By God's Grace, for God's Glory*, The Bible Speaks Today. Downers Grove, Ill.: InterVarsity, 2001.

Ryle, J. C. *Holiness: Its Nature, Hindrances, Difficulties, and Roots*. 1883. Reprint. Grand Rapids: Baker, 1979.

Sanderson, John W. *The Fruit of the Spirit*. 1972. Reprint. Phillipsburg, N.J.: Presbyterian and Reformed, 1985.

Sproul, R. C. *Faith Alone: The Evangelical Doctrine of Justification*. Grand Rapids, Mich.: Baker, 1995.

————. *Saved from What?* Wheaton, Ill.: Crossway, 2002.

Stott, John R. W. *Basic Christianity*. 2nd ed. 1971. Reprint in hardcover. Grand Rapids, Mich.: Eerdmans, 1999.

————. *The Cross of Christ*. Downers Grove, Ill.: InterVarsity, 1986.

White James R., *The God Who Justifies*. Minneapolis: Bethany House, 2001.

# Index of Scripture

225

**Carol J. Ruvolo** has been teaching the Bible since 1983 and writing books on biblical themes since 1998. A long-time resident of Albuquerque, she now speaks at women's conferences and retreats around the country.

Ruvolo earned B.S. and M.B.A. degrees from the University of New Mexico. Since 1996 she has taken graduate-level courses at Greenville Presbyterian Theological Seminary and several courses from Ligonier Ministries of Canada's School of Theology.

Though a devoted church-goer from childhood, she did not experience God's saving grace until she was an adult. Soon after her conversion she quit her job at a national defense laboratory and began devoting her time to raising her daughter and studying the Scriptures.

During the two years she participated in Bible Study Fellowship, she taught for the first time and soon realized that teaching is her spiritual gift. She says, "I have been teaching, counseling, discipling, and writing about God's revealed truth ever since."

Her published works include several volumes in the Light for Your Path series—which treats topics in Christian living and studies books of the Bible—and three studies on the book of James.

Carol is married and has one child.